WALKING
THROUGH
ANGER

WALKING THROUGH ANGER

a new design
for confronting
conflict in an
emotionally
charged
world

CHRISTIAN CONTE, PHD

sounds true
BOULDER, COLORADO

Sounds True
Boulder, CO 80306

This book is not intended as a substitute for the medical recommendations of
physicians, mental health professionals, or other health-care providers. Rather, it is
intended to offer information to help the reader cooperate with physicians, mental
health professionals, and health-care providers in a mutual quest for optimal well-
being. We advise readers to carefully review and understand the ideas presented
and to seek the advice of a qualified professional before attempting to use them.

Some names and identifying details have been changed to protect the privacy
of individuals.

Published 2019

Cover design by Lisa Kerans
Book design by Beth Skelley

Printed in Canada

Library of Congress Cataloging-in-Publication Data

Names: Conte, Christian, 1973–, author.
Title: Walking through anger : a new design for confronting conflict in an
    emotionally charged world / Christian Conte, PhD
Description: Boulder, CO : Sounds True, [2019]
Identifiers: LCCN 2019013299 (print) | LCCN 2019014126 (ebook) |
    ISBN 9781683643289 (ebook) | ISBN 9781683642589 (pbk.)
Subjects: LCSH: Interpersonal conflict. | Conflict management.
Classification: LCC BF637.I48 (ebook) | LCC BF637.I48 .C655 2019 (print) |
    DDC 158.2—dc23
LC record available at https://lccn.loc.gov/2019013299

10 9 8 7 6 5 4 3 2 1

TO EVERYONE WHO READS THIS:

May these words bring
you much peace.

Contents

Foreword by John Wetzel

Some of the angriest places in the world, and certainly in America, are inside prisons.

I was introduced to my friend Dr. Christian Conte through a congressman who asked me to meet with someone who had an answer for the problems in corrections. That type of framing obviously enhanced my already significant skepticism.

I remember that meeting like it was yesterday—I walked into a hotel restaurant early in the morning in Pittsburgh, and there's this bald, bearded dude in a shirt and tie who couldn't have looked more uncomfortable. He was clearly hiding a plethora of tats, reinforcing my skepticism.

Five minutes later, not only did I buy in, I also realized that this bald, tatted, Harley-riding dude was not only a kindred spirit in my quest to humanize conditions in prisons but a brother in every sense of the word.

However, I am charged with ensuring responsible spending of the taxpayers' dollars, so when he explained what he wanted to do, I did what anyone would do—I said, "Sure, doc, we'll try your Yield Theory; however, *prove it works*. I then gave him the most restrictive housing unit in my system. The Special Management Unit (SMU) program is designed for incarcerated individuals who have accumulated so much disciplinary time for acts of violence within the walls that it is unlikely that they will ever be released to join the rest of the population.

What happened next is nothing short of the most transformative thing I've seen in thirty years working inside of jails or prisons. Violence, complaints, and conflict decreased—communication and respect increased.

What's the secret sauce? Well, you have to read the book . . .

But it looks a lot like meeting people where they are in their life journey, validating where they are at without endorsing inappropriate behavior, separating your emotions from the situation, and acknowledging the commonalities.

Our officers are responsible for keeping the care, custody, and control of individuals locked up. Too often, mutual understanding isn't part of that harsh environment. Dr. Conte broke down the walls of communication so officers and inmates can see each other's humanity and created a space for respectful communication—and it worked!

John Wetzel
Secretary, Pennsylvania Department of Corrections

Foreword by Ron Potter-Efron

Introduction: The Value of Nonattachment

My wife Pat and I love minerals. We have perhaps five hundred different specimens at our house. One really special one is called okenite, a mineral best described as a bunch of fuzzy soft white spiky cotton balls. It is unusually fragile for a rock.

A few weeks ago, we had a friend (I'll call her Joey) and her friend (Billie) over for coffee. Naturally we wanted to show them our minerals. They loved them, but Billie unintentionally damaged the okenite by rubbing, and then did more damage when she seemingly ignored my request that she stop rubbing. She may just not have heard me, of course, but by then I was pissed off. I didn't blow up in anger, though. Instead, I simmered. Then I called Joey to complain about Billie with a predictable result: I significantly damaged and almost destroyed our relationship. The next day I sent Joey a note saying that I owed her an apology but hoped she'd understand that we loved our minerals almost like children or pets. A few days later Joey, Pat, and I talked things over. One of Joey's comments was "I walked around my house with my husband and I didn't find anything material there that I loved as much as my pets or children."

What a fortuitous time for me to be reading Dr. Christian Conte's new book. Indeed, I was just then starting chapter 6 on nonattachment. Conte writes in chapter 6 that suffering arises from desire. I would add that suffering arises from craving, holding on to material objects, and general possessiveness. He notes that the more attached you are to your own thoughts and feelings, the less able you are to hear and understand the thoughts and feelings of others. The point is that if I had loved my minerals without clinging to them, I would have maintained a sense of perspective. I'm not saying I would have thought, "Oh, no big deal, I care nothing about this mineral." Maybe in some future life I might say that. But I could have thought, "Damn. There goes my okenite. Too bad, but I can get more. Billie means no harm, so I'll stay calm."

Since I'm beginning at chapter 6, let me continue there, in part because I would recommend that unit if you were to read only one chapter from this book. Dr. Conte clearly relates nonattachment to anger management in the sense that the less we hang on to our beliefs, thoughts, feelings, and assumptions about the other, the more we will actually encounter that individual in a meaningful way. It is our attachment to these things that separates us from those with whom we are trying to communicate. Essentially, we must choose between nursing our cherished beliefs (as if they were our children) and fully engaging the other. To put it another way, we must give up the "I" of ego to discover the "us" of real connection.

Creativity and Personal Stories

The mark of a good book is an author's ability to present material in a distinctive and memorable manner. Think of Edgar Allen Poe's suspenseful buildups to terror or how Shakespeare makes you see his three witches as they hover over their caldron of evil potions. Here, in chapter 8, Dr. Conte offers his own distinct feature: helping angry clients learn from stories.

One critical way Dr. Conte uses creativity is to help clients not give their power away to others when they become angry. He uses a simple analogy: if your power were a solid object like a water bottle, would you hand it to the person you have just become angry with? Then he follows that up with several stories (some true, some metaphorical) of how people do exactly that, to their misfortune.

What Is Yield Theory?

Yield Theory represents the core concept that underlies this book. Dr. Conte has been discussing and describing Yield Theory for years at conferences we've attended. I must confess I only vaguely understood what he meant until now. Here, in his introduction and in chapter 1, Dr. Conte artfully describes Yield Theory as both a philosophy and an evidence-based model for change. Dr. Conte blends Eastern and Western awareness to help his clients (often extremely damaged, violent felons) see the world from the perspective of another, as opposed to their ego-driven, personal view of life. Practicing Yield Theory involves a "constant navigation" toward the position of the other. Practitioners will need to take three main actions: listening, validating, and exploring options. These always-difficult tasks will be eased by learning seven primary approaches to communication: acceptance, authenticity, compassion, conscious education, creativity, mindfulness, and nonattachment. Dr. Conte's goal as a counselor is to merge with his clients to guide them toward a path of non-resistance instead of constant anger, conflict, and aggression. More broadly, the goal of any reader who adopts Yield Theory as a model would be to lessen the grip of self-interest, self-focus, and self-pity—all of which distort one's understanding of the other—replacing these ego-driven pursuits with an undamaged perception of the other. Dr. Conte believes that most conflicts would dissolve, or at least be considerably subdued, by this effort. The reason is that ego destroys true connection. Ego makes merger impossible to achieve. Without merger, conflict is inevitable.

In 1961, Clark Moustakas wrote a wonderful little book entitled *Loneliness*. He described how people often suffered from what he termed "loneliness anxiety," the fear of being alone. Today we might diagnose some individuals with this condition as having a severe attachment disorder, a dread of living even a few moments alone. Many violent crimes have revolved around someone's inability to tolerate another person's need for distance. Moustakas contrasted loneliness anxiety with real loneliness: an unfearful, existential experience of the reality of one's inevitable separation from others. Do not be afraid of your loneliness, he wrote; instead, embrace it.

Yield Theory would appear to support a 180 degree opposite position. Here Dr. Conte enjoins the reader not to fear merger. He speaks to one's "natural" desire to protect and enhance our sense of self. No, he assures us, you will not be engulfed in the other's personality by merging with him or her. Instead, you will engage in a productive (and aesthetically enriching) exploration of a previously unknown shared universe.

You probably have anticipated my next comment. These two positions are not so unlike as they appear. For example, do you know how a psychologist would diagnose someone who has a dread of merger? He would say that person also has a severe attachment disorder, just like the person who dreads aloneness. It takes existential courage to withstand both the terror of isolation and the terror of merger. Dr. Conte makes the latter journey not only bearable but desirable.

How Yield Theory Works

In chapters 2 and beyond, Dr. Conte details how to apply Yield Theory in practice. Chapter 3, for example, focuses on the concept of acceptance. Acceptance of others is never easy. As I write this foreword just before the 2018 midterm elections, people are so of hate that they are sending bombs through the mail and invading synagogues with assault rifles. Many members of our society certainly don't appear ready to enter, much less travel through, the labyrinths of each other's minds. So, this is exactly the time Yield Theory needs to become widely understood and practiced. Something must happen, and soon, lest we destroy both each other and our society through hatred.

Dr. Conte emphasizes the need to validate others. He stresses that validation is only effective if the subject feels validated. Sensing when that occurs may well be what distinguishes excellent therapists from well-intentioned but ineffective ones.

The topic of chapter 4 is authenticity while chapter 5 is about compassion. These two concepts are variants of a similar theme: the need to be true to oneself in order to be truly available to others. This entails recognizing the tricks of mind which our egos make that inflate our self-centeredness at the expense of real connection and communion. Here Dr. Conte develops another excellent analogy, suggesting that we think of a sufferer as if he or she were dragging a heavy log. Our job is to walk over and pick up the other end of that log. That lightens our client's load just enough that he or she can "step back and ask themselves if they truly need to be carrying that log in the first place." Thus, compassion encourages reflection and reflection can alter the course of a person's life path.

My friend Charlie Rumberg tells a story about a man who became angry first with his kids, then his wife, and then with everybody else. When Charlie asked him to tell exactly what he was feeling before he became irate, this man answered: "I was hot." "Hot under the collar?" asked Charlie. "No, I had hot feet. I was wearing woolen socks and my feet were hot." That man's hot feet were the trigger for his anger. You might guess that he never did take them off during this nasty episode. That would have been way too simple a solution to his problems.

Dr. Conte writes in chapter 7, on conscious education, that your mind always tries to match your body state. That's one way we create our personal victim stories: since my feet hurt, somebody must be trying to hurt me. His point is that we can become better at gaining awareness of our physical being and thusly guard against the transformation of internal stress into external accusation.

Chapter 9 is the next-to-last chapter that remains to be discussed, on mindfulness. Dr. Conte begins with another wisdom story:

> A professor approached the Zen master and condescendingly asked him what made him a "master of Zen." The master said, "When I eat, I eat. When I walk, I walk. When I talk to someone, I talk to that person." The haughty professor, who could barely keep himself from interrupting the master, replied, "That's ridiculous! Everyone does those things! And I guess since I do them, that makes me a Zen master, too." The master smiled and said, "To the contrary, when you eat, you think of other things. When you walk, your mind is elsewhere. And when you talk to others, your mind is not on what they're saying, but on what you'll say next. You are anywhere but present. That is the difference."

Dr. Conte explains mindfulness well. He notes that we must strive to be mindful not only of our thoughts but also of our feelings, actions, physical presence, tone of voice, eye contact, posture, physiological state, and presence. In other words, mindfulness applies to our entire being and, to use a phrase from earlier in Dr. Conte's book, our essence itself. It is this complete approach to the concept of mindfulness that stands out as a significant addition to the standard literature on this topic.

Finally, Dr. Conte ends his volume with a chapter on what not to do. He describes five errors of communication: approach, interpretation, judgment, language, and omnipotence. Although useful, I would recommend you read these over and then return to chapter 6 on nonattachment before you complete your reading. It is in this chapter that the merger Eastern and Western approaches to anger management and life itself is best presented.

Ron Potter-Efron, MSW, PhD
author of *Angry All the Time* and *Letting Go of Anger*

If you want to be given everything,
give everything up.
LAO TZU

Introduction

Imagine you were trapped in a room and didn't see a way out. If people on the outside talked at you about how they got out of a room before, you'd likely feel pretty defensive. You might even be especially upset if they didn't realize that you were trapped in a completely different kind of room with an altogether different escape route than the one they were once trapped in.

"I'm in a different room!" you shout.

"Yes," someone replies, "but this is what I did to get out . . ."

"Please help me! I'm not in the room you were trapped in!" you respond.

"Well, I felt like that once too," another person on the outside says. "Let me tell you about how I felt . . ."

"I don't want to hear how you felt!" you say in desperation. "You telling me how you felt does nothing to help me get out of this room!"

"What's wrong with you?" a third person says. "Why are you so angry and resistant? We're all only trying to help!"

Because they can fully comprehend only their own experiences and the solutions that worked for them, the people on the outside genuinely don't understand why their words aren't helpful. And because the people on the outside don't take the time to listen to you describe what the room you're in looks like from your perspective, nor do they own the role they play in their interaction with you, they put the blame entirely on you.

And after all their words, there you are, still trapped in that room. Yes, there is a way out, but the people preaching at you about their experiences won't help you find it. You need solutions that will work for you, and you need those solutions to be relevant to the room you're actually in, not entirely different rooms that others were stuck in previously.

If you can feel the frustration of being in that scenario, if you can see clearly how ineffective it is for people to assume that you being trapped in a room is exactly the same as the experience they had, then you understand the key to circumventing defensiveness in communication. If you truly understand this scenario, in fact, I would argue that you understand why Yield Theory® is revolutionary and transformative. The room in the scenario is ever changing, as is the way out. Only one person can ever be in the room at a time, so no one else in all of time will ever see the room the exact way that you see it. And neither will you ever see the exact room others are in. All we can ever do is hear about each others' rooms.

The rooms are our psyches.

If you want to help people who are trapped in their rooms, there are three things that you can do. You can listen with humility as others teach you about their rooms. You can validate the experience and emotions they're describing. And then you can explore realistic options of what they can do to help themselves from this moment forward.

To do those three things well, it's crucial first and foremost to recognize where people actually are and then to be authentic in your desire to learn what they're willing to teach you about their experience. When you have the humility to lead with compassion instead of ego, you improve your chances of tapping into the creative processes that will help you shine a light of conscious education for others in a way that specifically addresses their individual needs.

Through it all, be mindful about the role you play in every inter-action, including what is and isn't in your control. The less attached you are to needing others to see what you see or having things go a certain way, the more you will genuinely help others help themselves to be free.

This is Yield Theory. ◀

Everyone has a story. Everyone. No matter the pain others cause, no matter the impulsivity they display, the mistakes they make, or any-thing else, there are no monsters among us; there are only human beings who have personal histories. That doesn't mean, of course, that people don't do terrible things, and it certainly doesn't excuse any harm that's done. Explaining behavior never excuses it, but it does help us understand it. Ultimately, just as in your own life, each moment has led to the next in the story of everyone's life. The more you understand those stories, the more effective you'll be at walking through conflict.

I specialize in anger management, and my path has often placed me right in the middle of some extraordinarily intense situations. Through the years, I have witnessed extremely effective and also terrifyingly ineffective approaches to handling anger. I've watched firsthand just how much anger can beget anger and how ego can escalate it; and I've also seen just how powerfully transformative and de-escalating a process I call "leading with compassion" can be. I learned that trying to see the world through other people's eyes requires only a shift in perspective, and it actually doesn't take any more time than not trying to do so. Having a nonjudgmental atti-tude doesn't mean not acting to de-escalate conflict and speak up, either. To the contrary: I will show you how leading with compassion and seeking to understand will help you navigate clearly and directly through even the most difficult and emotionally charged situations.

As I reflect on my own story, I can recall two distinct moments from my childhood that ultimately led me to becoming an expert in anger. I invite you to take a guess what those two events might be. My guess is that neither of these experiences is likely to be anything close to what you might imagine. And that's the point. The more you hear of individ-uals' stories, the less you assume, and the more you understand. More understanding leads to more effective communication, including in the handling of difficult interactions. Back to my story: Here are those two specific moments that I believe led me to choose the path I took all the way to the publishing of this book. See if your guesses were right.

My dad was a professor of English literature before he changed directions and switched to teaching earth science. When I was young, I saw the fun in storytelling, in mythology, and in the subject of literature; but, admittedly, I did not see the value in studying the ground. As a haughty teenager, I asked my dad why he chose to be an earth scientist. He replied, "If you're only ever going to live on one planet in your life, don't you think you ought to know about that planet?" I loved that answer. A few years later, when I entered college, I felt lost and didn't know what course of study to follow. I thought about my dad's explanation of why he did what he did. Then the thought occurred to me: I will only ever live with me, so shouldn't I get to know myself? I decided then and there to study psychology.

My mom was a high school English teacher. She was well respected among the students, because she was a strict disciplinarian. She was the kind of teacher kids tend to complain about as too demanding, only to realize as young adults that they benefited from meeting her requirements. The kids at the high school I attended had fistfights fairly frequently; like in any 1980s teen movie, the students really would circle up around the two kids who were about to duke it out. Before I entered ninth grade, my mom looked at me and said, "I had better never find out that you ever watched a fight. If you see people fighting, step in and break it up." I did as she taught me. From the time I was young, when I saw conflict, I stepped toward it, not away from it.

I didn't run from conflict then, and I don't run from it now: not others' and not my own. Learning about human behavior—about myself—and being willing to step toward conflict taught me simple but profound life lessons. Anger is natural, it's usually driven by ego, and we're not "wrong" or "bad" for feeling it; but we can certainly face regrettable consequences when we react to it impulsively. Perhaps the most awakening truth about the emotion of anger I've discovered is this: Regardless of how overwhelming anger ever feels or how scary conflict ever gets, *it will eventually pass*. In facing the conflict in my own life, I learned a great deal about myself, and the more I learned about me, the more effective I became at handling the anger I experienced. Eventually, I became effective at handling other people's anger, as well.

Now think about the guesses you made regarding the two experiences that shaped the direction I took. Were your guesses accurate? How on point were your assumptions? More importantly, after reading about my experiences, has your mind raced to convince you that what you thought was "pretty much" what I said? In other words, did you try to fit the answers I gave into what you thought they would be?

The way you respond to information that you didn't see coming says a lot about where you are in the process of personal growth. The more open you are to taking in new information, the closer you are to handling anger and conflict well. Conversely, the more your ego works to make the world fit into what you already know, the more prone you are to defensiveness and anger.

Being willing to face conflict effectively takes knowledge, self-awareness, and practice. The more you know about yourself and about how to handle highly charged situations, the more confident you'll be in handling them without allowing your own energy to be changed by them. This book will give you the keys to self-awareness, the knowledge for handling conflict, and the specific methodology to practice to get you to where you want to be.

Intelligence is knowing information, but wisdom is practicing it. It's great to understand intellectually that attachment to ego is at the heart of many episodes of anger and conflict. But being aware of what triggers your ego and understanding how to set your ego aside take effort. If you are attached to needing others to think, believe, or behave in the ways you expect (or demand), you will struggle to resolve conflict. In fact, the extent to which you are attached to needing things to be the way you demand them to be is directly correlated with how much anger you will experience.

As you will discover in this book, the Buddha's teachings have had a deep impact in my life and are interwoven throughout my approach. For example, in the Buddha's famous Fire Sermon, he talked about all things being on fire. The sermon can seem strange—here is a peaceful figure describing such burning and chaos—until you understand that the fire he described is *change*. Seeing the "fire of anger" in the context of change taught me to walk directly through it without being afraid and without being burned, because the profound truth I learned was that *all anger, all conflict, and in fact all emotional experiences have a beginning, a middle, and an end.* They will inevitably change. Once I understood on the deepest level the true temporary nature of anger, I was significantly empowered to avoid making impulsive decisions in the beginning or middle of tough emotional experiences that I knew would ultimately come to an end.

You, like me, will experience anger in your life. You will also encounter others who are angry. You are the only person in your life you will always live with, and you are the only person you can ever control in any interaction you ever have. The more you understand what leads to what in the story of anger and the concept of nonattachment, as well as the temporary nature of emotions, the better you will understand yourself, and the more open you will be to learning exactly what you need to do to walk directly through anger. In this book, I lay out the methodology for how you can do that.

The Origin and Substance of Yield Theory

I created Yield Theory as my approach to psychotherapy twenty years ago. I've used it as a guiding force from which I have interacted with widely diverse clients: individuals struggling with the normal emotions of life, people dealing with very serious mental health issues, families suffering from interpersonal chaos, couples learning how to communicate, adolescents toiling with their ever-present angst, elite athletes competing on the world stage, celebrities coping with too much attention, men and women struggling with issues of intense anger, everyday people suffering in the throes of addiction, and some of the most violent criminals on the planet facing the consequences of their actions. My therapy work has taken me from the comfortable Zen setting of my private practice to national television shows to the deepest regions of solitary confinement in maximum-security prisons.

I have seen thousands of clients, practiced more than 20,000 hours of clinical therapy, run a mental health organization, cofounded a center for people convicted of violent crimes, and taught as a tenured professor at a major university. In everything I've done, Yield Theory has guided me, helping me to counsel, teach, communicate, and cope with experiences I've had.

Yield Theory is a powerful philosophy and an evidenced-based approach to change. It is also a way of life. It is not a panacea by any means, but it is a revolutionary model from which you can learn how to interact with others on a deep level and induce change in a quick, effective way. It can help you connect with people who are resistant to change, and it can guide you through successful ways to handle any conflict. Yield Theory has been demonstrated to work as a de-escalation tool to help even highly resistant inmates classified as the most violent in maximum-security institutions make a statistically significant reduction in their violent outbursts, so imagine how effectively it can help you connect with others and deal with conflict in your own world.

Although it's true that you cannot change others, only yourself, it's also true that you can have an impact. The key to affecting others in a way that ignites a change in them begins with you meeting people where they are, not where you think they "should" be. Unfortunately, the following Zen parable paints a fairly accurate picture of the way most people tend to hope to spark change in others.

▶ A fool once stood at the top of a mountain. Looking down, he saw that all the other people were at the bottom. He wanted the others to be standing next to him, and he began to get angry. He yelled and screamed at the people to stop going the wrong way, and he shouted over and over that they should be next to him on the mountaintop. But no matter how angry he got, the fact remained that the others were at the bottom of the mountain. They were too far way to hear even a syllable of anything he said. ◀

Often we read stories such as these and believe that the foolish protagonist is someone "out there." We don't realize that at times we also embody the very same characteristics. Everyone who has ever espoused an angry opinion on social media or in an Internet comment section has been, in that moment, the fool on the mountaintop. More close to home, consider how many times you've wanted others to change so badly that you found yourself preaching *at* them rather than talking with them. "Yes, but it comes from a place of love," you say, and of course it might; but that doesn't change the fact that if you speak *at* others instead of *with* them, you will likely not be heard. If you want others at the bottom of the proverbial mountain to hear you, then it's on you to have the self-discipline to leave the place where you are, climb down the mountain, and meet them where they are. "Yes, but I shouldn't have to do that all the time," you say, and that's a perfectly normal thought to have; but in the moments when you think that, you are most precisely like the man at the top of the mountain yelling down to others.

Going down to the bottom of the mountain creates the opportunity for you to address conflict directly and at its source, instead of staying far away from it, doing nothing effective about it, and hoping it magically changes.

In the following pages, you will learn about yourself, anger, and how you can handle conflict in the most effective way possible. You will learn how to lead with compassion and humility in order to bypass people's defensiveness and how to communicate in ways that get through to them, regardless of their emotional state. The methodology isn't complex, but it does require effort to practice. The more you practice it, the better you'll get at it, until eventually it will become a natural way of interacting for you.

Knowing how to yield is strength.
LAO TZU

Yield Theory

Compassion as the
Cornerstone of Communication

Twenty years of clinical experience have taught me that the world boils down to two kinds of people: people with issues and dead people. That means if you are currently alive, then you, like me, have issues. It means that everyone with whom you interact also has issues. And when issues collide, conflict arises. Conflict is a natural and frequent part of human interaction, yet for the most part, people seem to struggle immensely with how to handle it. In this book, I share with you the approach I created to help connect with others and walk directly through anger and conflict, which I call *Yield Theory*. Yield Theory gives you the tools to lead with compassion so that you can effectively get around other people's defense mechanisms and communicate with them in ways that are heard, regardless of what emotional state they're in when you interact. It teaches you to connect with others quickly and get to a deep place with them much faster than you ever thought possible.

It all begins with you learning about you, because you cannot escape living with yourself, and you are the only person over whom you will ever have complete control. I understand the term "Yield Theory" can sound technical or dry and academic. To the contrary: Whereas Yield Theory is a systematic and empirical methodology based on years of research and practice, it is also a practical, accessible approach to changing how you handle the conflict that you will inevitably encounter in life. Using Yield Theory's three-step model, stories about real people from my clinical experience, the ancient wisdom of Zen tales, and our latest scientific understanding of the brain, I'll share with you how you can change the way you communicate and handle conflict in every part of your life.

Yielding isn't about giving angry people everything they want; it's about meeting people where they are, setting your ego aside, and following others into the depths of who they are. As the father of Taoism, Lao Tzu, once said, "If you want to lead others, you have to learn how to follow." Since individuals alone hold the key to the door to their vast, inner, subjective selves, the only way through the minds of others is to follow their lead. To do so entails strength. Yielding does not in any way equate with giving in or condoning unwanted behavior, but it does involve having the confidence to recognize and own what you do not and cannot know, and it most definitely requires having the courage to fully let go of the things that you cannot control.

Everyone has issues, and everyone experiences anger to some degree. You do. I do. We all do. Learning to deal effectively with your own anger is a prerequisite to your being able to help guide others through theirs. So, yes, Yield Theory is a method of handling the conflict you encounter, but it is first and foremost a tool for you to handle your own anger. Of all the strategies that don't work in anger and conflict management, people not being able to demonstrate that they live their message tops the list. The self-righteous perspective of "Do what I say, not what I do" offers little help to others, especially those who are angry. It's like whispering instructions to people a mile away—they simply won't hear it.

Being heard requires listeners who are ready to hear, and whether individually or in a group, angry audiences with a lot to say do not make ideal listeners. Communicating clearly and effectively in the heat of conflict can feel overwhelming, but by showing you how to meet people where they are, merge with them in the energetic direction they are already going, and then lead them away from their rage, Yield Theory offers you a clear methodology of hope in the face of the seemingly impassable barriers of conflict and anger.

Compassion at the Core

The Buddha taught that anger will never be overcome by anger—only by love alone. But how can you actually overcome anger with love? When I was young, I heard the metaphor about not judging others until you've walked a mile in their shoes, and that thought resonated with me. As I developed Yield Theory, however, I began to realize that walking a mile in someone else's shoes is not enough to enable me to truly understand another person. I asked myself this question: What if I lived every single day as that person? The more I thought about it, the more I realized that it would be logically impossible to say that, had I lived as others, I might have made different decisions. In other words, if I had other people's cognitive abilities, affective range, and life experiences, I believe I would have made every single decision they made. Of course, there really can be no proof one way or the other, but I found that subscribing to this idea helped me wipe away my judgment of people, be fully present with them, and consistently lead with compassion. Genuinely trying to see the world through other people's eyes is how I believe that we can overcome anger with love.

Compassion, then, is the foundation of Yield Theory. You might think it strange that someone who specializes in working with people convicted of violent crimes would be so passionate about leading with compassion. The following true story might give you a better sense of the perspective I have regarding both why I believe people hurt each other in conflict and why I believe that compassion is so important.

The Labyrinth: Why People Hurt Each Other

When my daughter, Kaia, was in second grade, she came home upset because another girl in her class had said something mean to her. Kaia was taken aback by what this girl said, mostly because she had a difficult time understanding why anyone would say something mean to someone else. We went into our meditation room, and I taught her a lesson that has become the cornerstone for how we view people who hurt others.

I took her over to the glass coffee table, knelt down beside it, and told her to imagine that there was an entire world of little people inside this table. "Now let's imagine that the world inside here is a giant labyrinth," I said. "Can you see it?"

With the beautiful imagination of a second grader, she said, "Yes, I can see it."

Next I said, "Okay, now let's pretend that the whole labyrinth is covered in complete darkness, but you and I have magical goggles on, so we can still see, even though everyone in the maze is in complete darkness. Can you see it?" Once she said she could picture it, I continued. "So with all these people moving around in complete darkness in a labyrinth, some people will bump into each other and hurt each other, right?"

"Right."

"Let me ask you something: Should you and I be upset with these people for bumping into each other and hurting each other?"

She said, "No."

"Why not?"

She said, "Because they just can't see." And that, of course, was my point, so I smiled lovingly at her and said, "You know, that's exactly what I think happened with that little girl today. She just couldn't see how much she hurt you."

To this day I think that's true for the rest of us as well. We hurt each other because we are all at times lost in a labyrinth. People have hurt each other and people have hurt you because they were lost in darkness. To recall the Buddha's teachings again, he said it's not your job to light up the entire world, just your corner of it. In the context of the labyrinth metaphor, it becomes clear why I emphasize you learning about yourself (lighting up your corner), because in the process you will find that others gravitate toward your light, and they will even welcome it in times of anger and conflict. It is the person carrying that light who can lead others out of a dark labyrinth.

▶ A blind man was leaving his friend's house when his friend handed him a lantern to carry home. The blind man said, "I don't need a lantern! I'm blind!"

His friend said, "The lantern isn't for you, it's so that others can see you." So he took the lantern and went on his way.

Sometime into his walk, a man bumped into him, and the blind man fell to the ground. He said angrily, "What's the matter with you! Can't you see this lantern?"

But the stranger said compassionately, "Brother, your light burned out," and he helped the blind man to his feet. ◀

Yield Theory entails first and foremost looking at the role you play in every interaction (making sure your light is on). It involves you being mindful of and in control of your own energy. Then it requires you to make the effort to meet others where they are and lead with compassion as you try to see the world through their eyes. The more self-knowledge you have and the more willing you are to accept full responsibility for your thoughts, feelings, and actions, the brighter your light, and the easier it is for you to get through the darkness. With your light shining brightly, you have a strong chance to help others see through the darkness as well.

Why It's Important to Walk Through Conflict

Although some people appear to thrive on conflict and even seem to create it when none exists, the more common phenomenon is that we, as human beings, do not like conflict, and so we either go to great lengths to avoid it or just flat outright handle it poorly. The reason we don't like it is that conflict brings up anger, and anger can lead to violence, and violence threatens our very existence. Our brains, via our amygdalae (the part of the brain that produces our fight-or-flight response), tend to make that unconscious connection between conflict and violence for us, whether we want them to or not.

If we were to view our species as an alien might, we would observe that the majority of people engage in games just to avoid experiencing conflict. Games can include ignoring others, giving in to them when we don't want to, meeting anger with anger in hopes of lessening anger, making concerted efforts to escape being around others, or even creating alternate smaller problems just to get away from the bigger conflicts that we perceive to be most difficult. Perhaps the most common way people avoid conflict is by stuffing their feelings deep down inside, which almost always results in their emerging somewhere else, usually in places that had nothing to do with the conflict's origins. You don't need to be a trained psychologist to see that conflict conflicts us, and it doesn't take expert analysis to notice that we tend not to handle it well.

It makes sense on several levels that we would want to avoid conflict, but the most basic is this: In moments of discord, we are not experiencing peace. Whether we want it to be this way or not, however, an inescapable reality of life is that we have to go through conflict to get to peace. We must walk directly through anger, not try to stuff it down or outright avoid it.

Understanding that the road to peace often goes through conflict is not a new idea. Medieval Christian churches had gargoyles placed on the outside of their doors, not to ward off evil, but to represent the inevitable conflict each person has to face en route to the peace that was symbolized by the interior of the church. If the church interior held the key to peace for the believers of that faith, then the entrants needed to understand (even symbolically) that it would not be easy to get there.

Perhaps no more vivid example of facing conflict to get to the ultimate peace exists than in *The Tibetan Book of the Dead*, a Tibetan Buddhist guidebook to help the dying move past ethereal "gargoyles." Travelers to the next realm are told that they will encounter both beautiful gods and their worst fears. Should they choose the conflict-free path of the beautiful gods, the consequences will be rebirth at the lowest level, because the easy path is only a temporary escape. If, on the other hand, the dying have the courage to face their worst fears and approach their greatest conflicts head on, they will soon recognize those fears for what they are: illusions. This realization will help them reach Nirvana and break the cycle of suffering for good.

Spiritual imagery and gargoyles aside, it can be scary to handle conflict; but the unfortunate reality is that ignoring it won't make it magically disappear. Viewing it differently, however, can radically shift the way you approach it. Etymologically, the word "conflict" comes from the Latin *conflictus*, which means "a contest." Viewing conflict as competition necessitates the existence of a winner and a loser, a paradigm that adds the element of me versus you or us versus them. Think of the implications of that. Fortunately, the etymology of "conflict" doesn't end with *conflictus*. *Con* means "together," and *figere* is "to strike," so "conflict" also means "to strike together"—a phrase that is not limited to meaning two or more striking together *against* each other; it can also refer to two people striking the same target *with* each other. From this perspective, conflict isn't about a winner and a loser, but about people joining forces to strike at a problem together. This is the Yield Theory interpretation of conflict: I am not in conflict against you. Rather, I am joining you in your conflict to help you strike upon the most effective solution possible.

Joining with others to walk directly through conflict is an essential part of this method. Yield Theory outlines a way for you to merge into anger and conflict in a direct but nonexplosive manner. The following metaphor of merging with others as the substance of Yield Theory came to me in 1998.

Imagine you were driving and noticed a man in another car headed down a dangerous and destructive road. To stop him from going that way, you would have several options, but let's say that only two came to mind. You could ram your car head on into his, which would indeed stop him from going down that road but would also end up damaging both of you greatly. So you scratch that idea.

The second idea is to turn around and drive in the same direction as him on the highway. You could yield to and then merge with him, pulling up next to him. Since this is a hypothetical scenario, let's say that he sees you are headed in the same direction and invites you into his car to save gas (jumping from car to car is entirely realistic in my made-up scenario). Now, from the front seat of his car, you are seeing things out of the same windshield, and you begin to have a clearer understanding of why he is headed in the direction he's going. Eventually he tires and asks you to drive for a bit. Now you can steer the car in a safer direction.

This metaphor of merging with others rather than resisting them is the substance of Yield Theory. Rather than stopping others' energy, you merge with it, and from the inside out, you help them change direction. As I have refined Yield Theory through the years, I've found the more accurate way of describing the final part of the original metaphor is merging with others to guide them into steering themselves down a different path.

The goal is not to resist the emotions people offer but to go with them and genuinely connect. It's not to avoid conflict or focus on where others "should" or "shouldn't" be but to meet them where they actually are. I studied the martial art aikido for many years (from *ai*, meaning "harmony," *ki*, meaning "energy," and *do*, meaning "the way"; often translated as "the way of harmonizing energy"). In aikido the goal is to maintain control of your own energy and redirect where others attempt to send you. In other words, if a person pushes you, instead of resisting and pushing back, you would yield and pull that person. Regardless of size, if you pull someone who is pushing you, you will easily be able to handle that person. The same is true if they attempt to pull you: You push. The push-pull philosophy means that instead of resisting, you go with the person.

In Yield Theory, the concept is the same: You do not resist the energy that others emote toward you in a conflict. Through nonresistance, you allow them to release whatever energy needs to come out so that they will be prepared to explore potential options with you. And just as in aikido you don't permit someone to hit you without redirecting that energy elsewhere, in Yield Theory, you never have to confuse not resisting someone's energy with tolerating their behavior. In fact, when you lead with compassion and nonresistance and listen to and validate others, much as in aikido, you will find yourself in control of the energy of the interaction.

In watered-down neurological terms, emotions are centered in the middle of the brain, whereas higher-level thinking and problem solving are largely centered in the front of the brain. Although that oversimplification likely makes neuroscientists cringe (because the reality is that the whole brain is widely interconnected in complex ways that we have yet to fully understand), the simplified visual is a very helpful tool for understanding communication. When people are emotional, angry, and caught up in the middle of their brain, it's difficult for them to think of alternative solutions to their current problem, and they tend to act impulsively. But when they are able to move out of that emotional state, they can both generate and take in viable, smart solutions. The key to handling conflict well is to help others get out whatever emotion needs to come out and then redirect them into the higher-level thinking and problem-solving region of their brain. Yield Theory helps you move others from one area of the brain to the other, and it enables you to do so expeditiously.

Everything at your disposal—from your presence to your energy to the types of words you use—can help you help others feel safe, and once people in conflict feel safe, they're more willing both to open up and to listen to feedback. When people believe that you can truly see what they see—or at the very least are trying your hardest to do so—it takes their openness to a whole new level.

Yielding to and going with others is neither a quick fix nor a one-dimensional concept. Yield Theory comprises three core actions and seven fundamental components. The three core actions understood in the context of the seven fundamental components will help you circumvent others' defensiveness and connect with them in a way that allows peaceful resolution and growth to be the goals of the interaction.

The *three core actions* are:

- Listen

- Validate

- Explore options

And the *seven fundamental components* are:

- Acceptance

- Authenticity

- Compassion

- Conscious education

- Creativity

- Mindfulness

- Nonattachment

Each of these core actions and fundamental components will be discussed in individual chapters, but it's important to understand overall that Yield Theory is a matter of practice rather than of intellectual knowledge. The fundamental components have to be understood to be practiced accurately. I use the word "components" to describe these foundational aspects of Yield Theory because they are not steps that need to be followed in a linear order; instead, they might best be pictured as minerals that, when combined and interlocked, create a very strong and durable granite. In the same way that different pieces of granite might contain more or less of a particular mineral, some of the components of Yield Theory might play a more or less significant role for different individuals at different times, but they are all necessary. Also, similar to granite, the components of Yield Theory often overlap. It's easy to argue that acts of compassion are also acts of mindfulness or that being nonattached is living out conscious education. The point is that, ultimately, the interconnection and overlapping of the components create great strength.

The following chapters will show you how using the three core actions in conjunction with the seven components, or *practices*, will provide you with a clear methodology for communicating with others, regardless of what state of mind and being they're experiencing.

How Yield Theory Works

Listen, Validate, Explore Options

The elegance of Yield Theory lies in its simplicity. It works by teaching us how to meet people where they are, connect with them without triggering their natural defenses, and give direct feedback in ways that they can actually hear. It never involves you trying to prove that you're right, but instead keeps you focused on attempting to understand what others are seeing and feeling, then continually improving the way you communicate.

The core actions of Yield Theory are to listen, to validate, and to explore options. That's it. Yield Theory is intentionally straightforward, because in the midst of anger and conflict, the last thing you want to do is try to recall a long, complicated list of bullet points and esoteric concepts. It's pragmatic, effective, and quick.

The greatest actions in life—being kind, helping others, doing the right thing—are not complicated, but just because something is easy to understand doesn't mean that it's easy to do. Think about martial arts. If you break down the essence of what even the greatest martial artists in the world do, it's three things: move, block, and hit. Although just about anyone might intellectually understand the concepts of moving, blocking, and hitting, the way someone like the legendary Bruce Lee actually performed those three actions was absolutely masterful, disciplined, and rooted in a sound system of delivery. So, yes, technically all you do when you're implementing Yield Theory is listen, validate, and explore options, but *how* you perform those three actions makes all the difference.

A recurring message you will encounter in this book is that *whatever you practice, you master*. Whatever you do repeatedly, such as acting impulsively, lashing out in anger, or allowing your emotions to get the best of you, you will master. Just the same, you can practice and master self-awareness, patience, and self-control. You can choose what to practice and therefore what you will eventually master.

Step One: Listen

A great deal of conflict is created and perpetuated by people not listening, so the first and perhaps most crucial step in Yield Theory is to listen. Simply saying the word "listen" isn't enough to help you understand how to listen effectively, however, because the way you listen is guided by your intention. If you listen, for instance, only to confirm what you think you'll hear, then your biases will inhibit your understanding. If you listen only to the content of the words others say, rather than taking into consideration how they're communicating those words, then that, too, will be ineffective. To listen effectively is to lead with humility and genuine curiosity, which reflects to others that you see they are communicating to you from a place you've never been and really want to know about—that is, their internal, subjective world, or their "room," to take the metaphor from the opening story.

The more active listening you do (for example, expressing verbal and nonverbal acknowledgment of what others say), the more you are able to focus on actually hearing what's being communicated to you. Listening is a skill, and skills can be developed. The following story is the cornerstone for how I teach the skill of listening.

The Box

▶ When my daughter was five years old, she came home from school one day and handed me a religious pamphlet someone had given her. The pamphlet reflected different beliefs from our own but stated, "This is the truth," so my daughter was confused. She said, "This has to be the truth, right daddy? It says it's the truth." So I took her upstairs to her playroom and had her lie down on her stomach on the floor. I put a big box in front of her and had her close her eyes for a minute while I put objects on each side of the box. She was close enough to the box that when she opened her eyes, she could see only one side of it.

When she opened her eyes, she saw a My Little Pony toy that I had set up on the side of the box she was facing. I asked her, "Is it true that there's a pony on this side of the box?"

She said, "Yes."

I said, "That's true, right?"

"Yes."

I then asked, "Is it true that there are little pony characters on every side of the box?"

She said enthusiastically, "Yes!" even though she couldn't see the other sides.

Then I had her slide over so that she could see two sides of the box. She discovered there wasn't another pony, but a little book leaning against the second side. She said, "Oh, I thought there would be a pony!"

I said, "That's okay, but is it still true that there's a pony on that other side?"

"Yes."

"Is it true that there is a book on this side?"

"Yes."

Then I asked her, "Is it true that there are probably a little pony and a book on the other sides of the box?"

And she said, "Now I don't know, because I can't see those sides." (I was blown away that a five-year-old had the insight to say this.)

I said, "Excellent!" Then I showed her that I had put two entirely different objects on the other sides. I asked her if seeing a book on one side made it any less true that there was a pony on the other side, and she said, "No." I continued, "It is true that there's a pony on that one side, and the fact that there are other objects on the other sides of the box doesn't make it any less true that the pony is still on that one side." I told her that the people who wrote that pamphlet and followed that path see their side of the box. "What they see might very well be truth to them, but it doesn't necessarily represent the truth of every side of the entire box." I told her that the more she understands that, the more she will see why people seem to feel so certain about what they believe. Regarding our own beliefs, I explained that even though we might believe there is no actual box, that, too, is only one perspective or side of the box.

I ended the lesson by quoting the opening lines of the Tao Te Ching to her: "The Tao that can be told is not the eternal Tao. The name that can be named is not the eternal Name." ◀ .

The lesson is one we since have named "The Box," and it is our go-to the moment people express different opinions or perspectives that don't seem to resonate or make sense to us. We simply say, "They are likely seeing a side of the box that we just don't see." We are not omniscient, nor are we supposed to be. Owning our limitations is a sign of humility, and it is the key to listening effectively. Recognizing that others are seeing a different side of the box doesn't make their side right and your side wrong (or vice versa); it merely helps you to understand the difference in perspective. It also helps us understand why people are so attached to what they believe. If they are standing right up against a particular side of the box, then what they are seeing from their perspective is true for them, which is why they feel so emotionally tied to it. Of course, if you believe that anyone with different opinions from you merely sees one side of the box, whereas you obviously see more sides, then you will allow your ego to inhibit listening effectively.

Listening to others as though they are seeing a side of the box that you cannot see is powerful. It's transformative. It's disarming. The reason why it's so important to listen to others as if they are seeing something that you simply cannot see the entirety of is that if they are talking about their own inner subjective worlds, the reality is, you absolutely cannot see the entirety of what they see. That's perfectly okay, because others cannot see the entirety of your subjective world either, which is also okay and natural. It's only our egos that try to convince us we need to "know" what others know. To listen to others as though they see a side of the box that you do not see is to operate from a position of curiosity and humility. When you want to see what others see, and when you genuinely believe that you need others to tell you about their side of the box in order to get a more complete picture, then you will listen openly to them in a way that lowers their defenses and helps them feel safe, which leads to de-escalation.

If you don't actively listen to the entirety of what others are communicating, you can miss the context and run the risk of not hearing the message. Thomas Edison recalled being a telegraph operator in Cincinnati on the night of April 14, 1865. He said there was a huge crowd gathering outside, and then they heard that President Abraham Lincoln had been shot. The boss told the operators to look over their files, and within a few minutes, a man held up a short account of the shooting of the president. The operator had written down the Morse code message without paying attention to the content of what it said. He "heard" without listening. Imagine taking down, "Lincoln's been shot!" but not notifying anyone because you weren't really listening to the message.

Flash forward to your own life. Let's say you're interacting with a friend you know well, and that person says something derogatory and inaccurate about you. The more immersed you are in the literal words that are said, the more you miss the larger message and the context in which it's being delivered. Maybe your friend is struggling immensely, and she lashes out at you because she feels close enough to you that she believes you won't abandon her if she does. In reality, she could be suffering about something that has nothing to do with you and displacing her pain onto you. Understanding where she's coming from or why she's saying what she is doesn't justify it or excuse it, but it can certainly help you take it less personally and therefore react differently to it. The more you can step back and be open to seeing additional sides of the box beyond your own, the more likely you are to be able to actually see more sides. From a larger perspective, you will have a better chance to hear more than the literal words that are spoken and look at a significantly bigger picture.

Expressing interest in others is one of the greatest entryways to connection we can ever establish. In times of conflict, our instinct often leads us to putting up walls (defenses) to protect ourselves. In fact, when you're directly involved in conflict (and not just intervening to lessen others' conflicts), your defensiveness can inhibit you from wanting to listen to or understand others' perspectives, and understandably so; but Yield Theory is predicated on genuine connection and understanding. It's about setting aside your ego (the only psychological aspect you're actually protecting in an argument) and operating from your essence. To listen accurately to others, it's important to wipe away as many of your own barriers as possible; otherwise you're listening only for what you want to hear, and you will be too clouded by your biases to actually hear others.

Listening well involves being present, open, and attentive to what others communicate in the moment. The more you focus your energy on being present, the more you can listen with genuine curiosity, rather than getting caught up in what was previously said, listening for what you believe others might say in the future, or—perhaps even less effective—listening for others to stop talking so that you can speak.

One way to be fully present with others and seek to see what they see from their side of the box is to pay attention to the multiple means they use to convey information. People communicate just as much with their body language, facial expressions, and tone of voice as they do with their words. One of the first lessons counselors in training learn is the difference between content and process. *Content* comprises the actual words people say, whereas *process* reflects how they say them. To practice discerning between the two, visualize summarizing in one word what people are expressing. For example, regardless of how many words a person might espouse in a given outburst, their one word might be "anger" or "helplessness" or "fear" or "concern." Think of how frequently the words "I said I'm fine!" have been used in conflict: The content might indicate that the person is okay, but the process obviously suggests they are "hurt" or "upset."

When you learn to "listen with your eyes" as well as with your ears, you'll improve your ability to truly hear immeasurably. By observing others, you will have an opportunity to pick up on the energy they are exuding, which is one of the most effective ways to listen. The more you are able to pick up on the incongruence between people's content and their process, the more accurate validation you can offer in step two. If you want to learn to listen well, the first step is to step back and see others. Yes, there will absolutely be times when the content of what people say is more significant to hear than the process of the way they're saying it, but as a general rule of thumb, especially in situations of conflict and anger, it's usually pretty safe to at least start off by paying close attention to process.

So to listen effectively: Start by assuming others are communicating to you from a side of the box you can't see, and then do your best to set your ego aside and try to see what they're seeing from their perspective. Then, with genuine curiosity, watch or listen for tone in the way they communicate and deduce a one-word hypothesis. Once you do that, you'll be prepared to test what you think you're hearing them communicate in the second step.

Step Two: Validate

To check whether you get what others are saying (that is, your accuracy of listening), the next step is to validate others. Validation involves acknowledging how people feel or verifying that you understand what they're communicating. To validate is not to condone what others are saying or support what they're doing; it's simply to communicate that you understand, to the extent that you can, what they're expressing about their subjective feelings and perspectives. That's it.

To validate others, you might say things along the lines of the following phrases. (These phrases are meant to suggest general concepts—the specific words and vernacular have to be authentic and true to you.) The tone of how you communicate makes a world of difference, so as you read these phrases or practice saying them out loud, do so with the utmost compassion and genuine concern.

- You seem really upset . . .

- You seem furious . . .

- It sounds like you feel this in your whole being . . .

- It sounds like you feel pretty hurt . . .

- It sounds like you're really frustrated . . .

- That has to hurt . . .

- I can't imagine every aspect that must be
  going through your mind . . .

- It's like this is so overwhelming that it's the only
  thing you can even think about right now . . .

- I can see you're frustrated that I don't seem to be
  getting what you want me to be getting . . .

- You seem disappointed, too . . .

(Anytime you add a word like "too" 'or "also" at the end of a validation, you minimize the desire for others to correct your exact wording,
and you also give them an opportunity to clarify. So they might say in
response, "I might be disappointed, but mostly I'm just blown away
that they would do that.")

Of course, these are just some examples of what you can say to offer
validation, and they're framed in the way I speak, but the underlying
idea is what's important: Acknowledge how others feel. The tone of the
way you validate is extraordinarily important. For example, because I
visualize myself so completely from behind others' eyes, I often say the
phrase, "That sucks" as a validation, but my tone is entirely sincere,
as I imagine I am joining with their mind and saying it from their
perspective.

You could conceivably say all of those statements above in a sar-
castic or harsh tone, and that would not be validating at all. If you
say them with authentic humility and compassion, however, each of
those statements is a powerful way of showing others that you get

what they're communicating or, at a minimum, are trying to get it. Remember, validation confirms to others that you hear what they're communicating, so if your tone doesn't match humble curiosity and isn't reflective of you leading with compassion, then it's unwise to expect that your reflections will help de-escalate conflict.

As you will see, one of the most crucial factors in Yield Theory is nonattachment. In validation, practicing nonattachment will help you stay open to listening to others' perspectives from different sides of the box. In literal terms, that can mean you being open to being corrected at all times. The less attached you are to the statements of validation you offer, the easier you will make it for others to clarify what they're trying to express and, ultimately, the more likely they are to feel validated. Nonattachment allows you to avoid adding to conflict, because the energy of a nonattached person is much safer to be around than that of someone who demands you fit into their preconceived vision of where you "should" be. In addition, with nonattachment guiding validation, your focus doesn't have to revolve around constantly clarifying what you meant; instead, it can stay centered on trying to understand others.

Imagine coming home to a loved one who gives you little eye contact, has closed-off body language, and sighs exhaustingly, but when confronted says angrily, "I'm not upset!" You can challenge that response and say, "Yes, you are!" which has the potential to lead to your loved one defending the "I'm not upset!" statement. Or you can yield to the defensiveness and say something along the lines of, "Okay. I'm really sorry I misread that. I would love to know what's going on, though, because it seems from your body language like something's going on."

The goal is not to be right, but to understand. Angry people often operate out of defensiveness, but validation can offer a powerful key to getting around that defensiveness. When you validate, you are able to confirm whether you are accurately hearing and understanding what others want to convey. We are deep and complex beings, and our minds are vast spaces of subjective experience, so knowing that others are at least understanding what we're communicating is incredibly important for connection.

Accurate validation can at times, in and of itself, provide a sense of healing for others, because it's a relief to know that someone else gets us, especially when anger or pain is clouding our ability to communicate clearly. Our inner subjective worlds can be lonely places, and when we feel like others cannot understand where we're coming from (our side of the box), that feeling of isolation can contribute to additional anger and conflict.

Since your perspective drives your approach, I think it's important to understand just how deeply ingrained our desire to connect with one another is. Although we all could use our space from time to time, and in times of conflict we certainly seem to want more distance from others than in times of joy, the reality is that none of us ever truly wants to be abandoned. So just because someone might want space, that doesn't mean the person doesn't want to be understood.

There is an anthropological theory that supports why we want others to get what we're communicating. In evaluating differences between Neanderthal and *Homo sapiens* brains, researchers discovered that Neanderthal brains had a larger portion devoted to vision and motor control and a smaller region devoted to social interactions. Combined with a genetic analysis demonstrating that Neanderthals lived in small, isolated groups that had little contact with each other, that information led to the hypothesis that *Homo sapiens* might have outlived Neanderthals because, to some degree at least, we instinctually recognized the power of the group. In other words, our far and distant ancestors likely realized that greater numbers meant better chance for survival. For the vast majority of the past 300,000-plus years of our existence as a species, being isolated from or kicked out of a group often meant death. So there is some evidence to suggest that perhaps our encoded genetic makeup is the real reason that, even if we do want time or space to ourselves, we tend to want it on our own terms and not have it be imposed on us. But you don't need anthropologists, psychologists, research, or experts of any kind to tell you what you've known since your very first experience of conflict: When you're angry, you want others to understand why. And just like you, so does everyone else.

Our drive for connection is the reason why solitary confinement is viewed as the harshest punishment that we can inflict on prisoners;

being forced to live in isolation is psychologically crippling. Within the framework of our complex neurobiological network is a deeply ingrained desire to avoid banishment from the group. In short, we're hardwired to need one another. Now, needing others for survival is not the same as needing them to understand our frustrations, but our brains' amygdalae don't discern between the two, and in times of conflict, no matter how angry people get, they still have that instinctual drive to connect, which often translates into a pretty strong desire to be understood. Although we might not ever be able to be *fully* understood (in chapter 10, I discuss the detriment of saying things like, "I completely understand"), the reality is that we very much want others to at least try to understand where we're coming from, especially when we're angry.

So people want you to be interested in what they're communicating, and in times of conflict, that desire to be understood is amplified. Sometimes people want to express their anger *to* you, and other times they want to express their anger *toward* you (the nonattachment component of Yield Theory teaches you how to avoid taking things personally). Regardless of whatever others want, the more you can listen accurately to what they're expressing and respect their right to feel however they do, the more emotionally safe they will feel around you, and the more likely it is that they will be drawn to connect with you. What I hope to be able to convey in writing is just how quickly that connection can happen when you approach others from a genuine place of nonattachment, nonjudgment, humility, and curiosity. The more others connect with you through your validations, the more they'll be prepared to explore options with you.

The challenge, of course, is knowing when to offer connection, when to back off, and when to move to the third step of exploring options. Again, the key to finding that balance lies in validation. To validate is to acknowledge where a person is emotionally. As you will see with the fundamental component of acceptance, knowing where people are emotionally (and intellectually) is critical to being able to meet them there. Because emotions are ever-changing states, assessing where others are is a constant process. For now, it's important to understand that the primary purpose of validation is connection.

The most essential rule of thumb, from a Yield Theory perspective, is to imagine yourself actually *being* that other person. The more you put yourself in others' shoes, the more authentic your validations will be. To improve how you validate, keep your statements fairly general (for example, "You seem really angry/hurt/frustrated/ disappointed . . ."). When you keep your reflections vague, you leave room for the other person to fill in the blank accurately. If you guess inaccurately at the emotion you're sensing, you're likely to add defensiveness or a feeling that you're just not getting what the person is saying. Plus being unattached to what you're perceiving can make others feel safe and more likely to open up to you. In fact, it's crucial to use less attached language for that reason alone. I tend to use phrases like "It seems like . . ." or "I wonder if . . ." or "It sounds like . . ." because the less certain I am with my language, the less rigid I am, and the more room I have for flexibility if the person tells me I'm off base. Because so much anger revolves around rigidity, approaching validation with a softness gives others little to resist.

There are reasons it's important to be open to being wrong. If you attempt to validate a highly resistant person, even if you are accurate, that person might tell you that you're wrong; not getting caught up in proving that you're right will circumvent that potential argument. Second, conflict causes confusion, and you cannot actually see into others' phenomenological worlds, so the truth is you might actually *be* wrong. Either way, approaching validation with humility is critical. When you're open to seeing that you might be wrong in your validation or that even if you're right the person might not be prepared to have their emotions identified just yet, then you remain in a position of continuously seeking to understand. Humble curiosity goes a long way in bridging gaps during conflict.

Since the primary goal of Yield Theory is to circumvent others' fight-or-flight response, perhaps the most important reason to validate is that it opens up a metaphorical valve through which a person's emotions can be channeled. Remember that when we're emotional, there is greater energy in the limbic system (the emotional center located toward the middle of our brains), specifically in the amygdala. When we're less emotional, that energy is freed up to move to the front part of our brain—the frontal cortex, the seat of our higher-level thinking and decision-making. The more we're in our frontal cortex (as opposed to the limbic system), the more prepared we are neurologically to explore as many options as we can. In other words, once you help angry people get their emotions out, they are much more ready to explore potential options of "where do we go from here" with you.

My golden rule in validation is this: *Do not just validate until you think the other person is validated; validate until the other person actually feels validated.* I call it "draining the limbic system." Imagine that a person's limbic system is filled with water and connected to a faucet. If you were to turn on the faucet only briefly, it wouldn't be long enough to drain all the water out. Imagine further that as long as there is water in the limbic system, the frontal cortex cannot work properly. So in order to help that person make better decisions, you would have to fully drain the limbic system. In other words, you cannot just turn the faucet on until you *think* the water is drained out, you have to leave it on until it actually *is* drained out.

It's tough to simultaneously defend what you're hearing *and* be open to listening. Understand that it's only your ego that wants to prove that you *did* validate the person; your essence is willing to continue to evaluate where that person is in each given moment. When you can approach conflict with the intention of genuinely wanting to listen to what others have to say, as well as make the effort to validate what they're communicating, your actions demonstrate that you're willing to set your ego aside in favor of the kind of listening that embodies compassion. Interestingly, you will find that the sooner others actually feel heard, the sooner they are likely to drop their defenses and the more quickly the interaction will move from striking *against* one another to striking *with* one another—to finding solutions, or what I call "exploring options."

Step Three: Exploring Options

Anytime we're emotional, we have a difficult time seeing the bigger picture. Think of it this way: If an object smashes into your shin and causes you physical pain, it's difficult in those next few moments to think of anything other than that shin pain. Likewise, when we're struggling emotionally, it's tough to see anything outside of whatever pressing emotions are present. This is especially true with anger. Anger narrows our focus. In the heat of conflict, we are significantly less likely to be able to see just how many options we have. That is why it's so important to actually circumvent people's fight-or-flight response, because the goal is to get to the place where you can actually figure out what to do from where you and they are.

Whereas listening and validating help break down and eventually release negative feelings, exploring options helps you direct people through the problem-solving aspect of the dilemma. The more intentional you are from the outset with the three core actions (with your primary goal being to connect with others and help them steer themselves down a different path), the easier it will be for you to avoid taking others' struggles personally. And the less personally you take other people's pain, the less defensive you'll be, which will make it easier for you to remain calm and centered. Then, in the act of exploring options, you can draw on every ounce of creativity you have to set up others to make less impulsive decisions and grow from the conflict at hand.

Probably the most important thing to know about exploring options is that no matter the number of realistic options people in conflict might have, the best strategy is to begin exploring the one that's immediately on the table. Even if the option seems extreme, if a person sees it as viable, then it's an option. Considering an option does not mean endorsing it. For example, if a teenager says he wants to punch his teacher in the face, then that's an option. It might not be the option I endorse, and there will certainly be consequences if he follows through with it, but nonetheless, I would not tell him that he cannot do that, because the reality is, it *is* an option. Denying it as an option would be the opposite of a Yield Theory approach. So I would explore his impulsive thought. I would listen to his perspective, validate his anger, and verbally play out what might happen if he followed through with his instinct. Punching his teacher is not what I would want him (or anyone) to do, so it's not in any way something I would condone, but I recognize that it's unwise to avoid acknowledging the reality of what someone is considering. As I join with him, however, he can start to drop his defenses and examine that impulsive, reckless option in a safe psychological space, opening himself to my helping him honestly evaluate that option. The more clearly he sees the future play out, the more likely he is to make a better decision.

Telling people that something they're thinking is not an option is invalidating, and telling angry people that something they're thinking is not an option actually only makes that option more tempting. We have an inherent drive to be free, so when we're told we cannot do something, it's a fairly common response to rail against that, especially if we're already feeling defensive or, worse, aggressive. Again, the goal of Yield Theory is to circumvent the fight-or-flight response, not elicit it, and if something's an option, it's an option, and the sooner you acknowledge it without judgment, the sooner you can explore the realistic outcomes of what might happen if the person follows through with it, as well as moving on to considering alternative options.

Exploring options completely expands the reach of Yield Theory. It's the space in which you can mindfully and creatively help to bring conscious education to others. When you're authentic and you accept others for who and where they are, and when you lead with compassion and are unattached to what you present others, people will be significantly more receptive to the conscious information you bring them. The core action of exploring options opens the door to presenting information from literally any angle. In subsequent chapters, I'll show you how you can draw on pragmatic techniques (from metaphors to practical strategies) that spark insight and change—and you'll see that all of them are applicable in the phase of exploring options.

Yield Theory's three core actions of listening, validating, and exploring options provide the fundamentals for approaching any conflict. In the next chapters we'll explore the seven fundamental components, or practices. As you fully integrate the seven fundamental components, you will see that Yield Theory is an extremely efficient approach that will help you connect with others quickly and move through conflict in an effective way. As with any other skill to master, practice is the key.

▶ Once a prominent leader went to a famous Zen artist and asked him to draw a picture of his beloved cat. The artist told the man to come back for the drawing in a month. When the statesman returned, the artist sent him away, saying that he wasn't ready and that he should come back after six months. Perturbed, but resolved to have a picture from this famed artist, the man went away. When he came back after six months, the artist again sent him away, saying he needed a full year to complete the task. Now this statesman was an important person, and important people don't like to wait, so he was visibly angry when he agreed to come back after a year.

When the man returned a year later, the artist said, "Okay, I'm ready." He pulled out a pencil and a blank sheet of paper, and in minutes he drew the most beautiful, striking, and perfect resemblance of the man's cat. The man was blown away by how beautiful the picture was, but he was more than confused as to why he had to wait so long when obviously this artist could draw such perfection in a matter of minutes. In fact, the more he thought about it, the more upset he got, until finally he angrily asked, "Why did you make me wait so long when it didn't even take you that long to do?" To which the Zen artist simply smiled and walked over to his closet door. When he opened it, out fell thousands of drawings . . . of cats. ◀

What takes moments to do in mastery has taken many more in practice. As with the master artist who drew thousands of drawings of the statesman's cat before he could draw the cat masterfully on the spot, the more you practice seeing the world through other people's eyes, listening, validating, and exploring options, the more effective you will be at doing so without much effort at all.

You don't have to wait until you face conflict to begin practicing the three-step process of listening, validating, and exploring options—or applying what you're about to learn regarding the seven fundamental components in the following pages. In fact, you can begin practicing seeing the world through other people's eyes right now and immediately increase your empathy.

Think about any one person in the world. It can be someone you love, someone who irks you to no end, or even someone you'll never encounter, but picture that person right now as clearly as you possibly can. Imagine what it might be like to be that person. Imagine what life experiences might have led that person to being in the exact spot where you're imagining them to be right now. Think, too, as though you are not only behind that person's eyes but also thinking with that person's brain. Imagine clearly all the life experiences that led to the moment that you are envisioning.

As that person, what do you see? As that person, what do you feel? Again, the question is not what you *want* the person to see or feel, but what you imagine that person actually does see and feel. This is the foundational exercise of Yield Theory. Like the master artist from the teaching tale, the more you practice attempting to see the world from other people's perspectives, the more quickly you'll be able to draw that picture in your mind from the instant you interact with them. The goal is not to eschew your own perspective in favor of others', but to understand clearly where others are coming from in every given situation.

Summary

The way Yield Theory works is straightforward: You attempt to see the world from others' perspectives and then listen, validate, and explore options. These three core actions are simple to articulate but take considerable intentional practice to master. To listen to others through the paradigm of Yield Theory is to imagine them on the other side of the box, to acknowledge that they are perpetually seeing a side that you cannot see (that is, their inner, subjective worlds), and to focus on constantly trying to understand. As you listen with genuine interest and humility, the next step is to validate, communicating what you think you hear others saying and confirming or adjusting your understanding through their responses. Once you have "drained the limbic system" of anger, you can move toward striking together with others to find the best possible solutions from the present moment forward. Listening, validating, and exploring options can help you walk directly through any conflict you encounter.

Acceptance

Meeting Others Where They Are

If your child's car broke down and she called to ask you to give her a ride, your first pragmatic question would be "Where are you?" Without knowing where she is, after all, how could you possibly go get her? You could, of course, spend time berating her about how she should have done things differently and why she shouldn't be where she is; you could even allow your ego to preach that she "should have listened" to you about the car she took in the first place, but none of that would do anything to actually change her current location. In fact, you announcing that you're "right" from your pedestal will not only *not* change where your daughter is, but it will also likely elicit her defensiveness and might even cause her to hesitate before reaching out to you the next time she needs help.

There is a better way to handle the situation.

Acceptance is the first fundamental component to Yield Theory. It centers on assessment. Specifically, acceptance refers to assessing what is happening, who is involved, and where people are in their understanding of a situation, as well as their willingness and preparedness to do something differently from what they're currently doing. The component of acceptance is the embodiment of meeting people where they are and seeing them as more than just the sum of what they've done. Acceptance does not in any way equate with allowing or even condoning any unwanted, ineffective, injurious, dangerous, violent, or abusive behaviors or speech. In accepting others, you do not have to compromise your values or ethics or avoid taking swift action. Instead, acceptance injects objectivity into what could otherwise be a highly charged subjective encounter.

Accepting What Is Happening

There is a difference between what I call the *cartoon world* and the *real world*. The cartoon world is the world as you demand it to be; the real world, on the other hand, is the world as it is. The difference is profound: one reflects your imagination, whereas the other reflects reality. The more you align your expectations with your cartoon world, the more you feel let down; but—and this is important to know—in truth the world is not letting you down, because the world is simply what it is. Instead, you are the one who is letting yourself down, because you are expecting the world to be something that it isn't.

When you align your expectations with reality, you are much more likely to see yourself and others exactly where they are physically, mentally, and emotionally. From the perspective of the real world, you are prepared to accept what is actually happening, as opposed to what you believe "should" or "shouldn't" be happening. Once you recognize the reality of what is happening, you can accurately meet others where they are rather than demand that they be where you want or magically expect them to be.

In her 1950 book *Neurosis and Human Growth*, psychoanalyst Karen Horney referred to the emphasis on an alternate reality of unrealistic demands as the "tyranny of the should." When I first read about that concept, I instantly thought of a cartoon picture of a huge, personified internal tyrant trying to angrily persuade me that the world is operating wrongly—hence my naming it the "cartoon world." Calling it the cartoon world is my lighthearted way of shining light on our world of shoulds.

"Things should go the way I want them to!"

"This traffic jam shouldn't be happening!"

"She shouldn't have said that!"

"He shouldn't have done that!"

"They shouldn't believe that!"

"He should know better!"

"She should have listened to me!"

"He should stop!"

The problem with the cartoon world, where the tyranny of the should rules, is that shoulds are opinions, not facts. That people should treat others kindly is a beautiful opinion, but an opinion nonetheless. The fact is that people do not always treat one another kindly, and, as A. E. Housman advised in his poem "Terence, This Is Stupid Stuff," "I'd face it as a wise man would, and train for ill, and not for good." When you are prepared for the reality that you face in life, you can equip yourself to handle it. To "train for ill" does not mean expecting everything to be awful all the time (or to expect the worst) either, because that is equally unrealistic. The inaccurate language of the cartoon world leads to unnecessarily heightened anger and angst, whereas the accurate language of the real world gives you a chance to assess exactly what is happening—which ultimately allows you to begin working on what you can change swiftly.

Psychology 101 teaches us that past behavior is the best predictor of future behavior. This doesn't mean that people cannot and do not change, but it does mean that without a motivation or an effort to change, people are more likely to continue in the same behavioral patterns that they've established. If, for instance, you have a friend who has divulged secrets you entrusted to him in the past, and you begin to tell him a new secret, then understanding the reality of what is happening—that is, you are entrusting a secret to someone who has shown you with his actions that he's not effective at secret keeping—helps you prepare to interact wisely. Aligning your expectations with reality means expecting others and the world to be, by and large, what they have shown you they are.

▶ Once, a viper was caught under a boulder that had rolled down a hill in a landslide. A man walked by, and the snake called out to him to move the rock. The man said, "No way! You're a deadly snake. You'll bite me, and I'll die." The snake said convincingly, "No, I won't. I promise!" And so the man moved the rock. The moment the snake was free, it instantly sunk its fangs into the man's leg, releasing its deadly poison. Furious, confused, and upset, the man asked in his last breath, "Why would you do that?" To which the snake replied, "I'm a snake. That's what I do." ◀

The man operated from his cartoon-world belief that the snake "should" keep its promise, even though the behavioral patterns of the snake taught him otherwise. Living in your cartoon world distracts you from handling the reality of the conflict in front of you. Convincing yourself that things shouldn't be the way they are is a psychological gargoyle that keeps you turned away from the actual conflict at hand. Operating from the real world, on the other hand, allows you to walk confidently through the reality of what's happening without placing unrealistic, self-created "shoulds" as obstacles in your own path.

Accepting Who Is Involved

Accepting who is involved in conflict begins with understanding, quite literally, which people are associated with a given situation. Although that might seem wildly obvious to state, the reality is that, oftentimes, people deny who is actually involved. For example, sometimes it's hard for parents to acknowledge the role their children play in conflicts with other children. Likewise, people who strongly identify with a particular group can struggle to see the role someone from their group plays in conflict with an opposing group. And beyond acknowledging others who might be involved in any given conflict, it's more important to understand that *you* are a part of every conflict in which you intervene (even if you're only intervening through others, as in giving advice).

Systems theory is one of the most empowering models for describing human interaction, because it states that everyone in a given system and interaction plays a role. That's not to say that people *cause* others to do anything, but that from an objective perspective, each person in an interaction plays a role. Think of characters in a movie: Even the thought of encountering background characters can influence the way the main characters move and interact ("We have to be quiet—someone might be here"). Recognizing that you in fact play a role in every interaction you have is empowering because it helps you focus on controlling the only person over whom you actually have control: you.

So if your friend comes to you to ask for insight about a conflict she's having with her partner, you are now playing a role. Even if you say absolutely nothing, your silence or your physical reaction will have some impact on your friend, and she might use some piece of her interaction with you in formulating her next move. In other words, as long as you interact with other human beings, you are a part of the system. I've watched clients in family therapy say to one another, "I don't want to be involved! I'm not saying anything." To which their loved one replies angrily, "Yeah, you won't even help me, which is why I do this on my own!" Then, "being left out to dry" becomes integrated in the loved one's narrative. The point is that it doesn't matter if you didn't ask to be involved or don't want to be—the reality is that you are. As long as you live, you cannot escape your participation in life; how you participate, however, is entirely up to you. Accepting your involvement allows you to have the most conscious impact possible.

When you recognize the role you play—including identifying your expectations, the internal or external demands you make, and whether your impact is direct or indirect—you can begin to ask yourself three key personal-growth questions that will help you reflect on all of your interactions.

1. What did I do effectively?

2. What did I do ineffectively?

3. What can I do more effectively next time?

Notice that none of these key questions center on judgments regarding who you are; instead, they are focused entirely on assessing your level of effectiveness in a given situation. As with practicing seeing the world from others' perspectives, the more you practice asking yourself these three questions after your interactions, the more they become second nature to you, and the faster you can identify answers to each. Remember, Yield Theory begins with you learning about you. Your ability to handle conflict well will increase in direct proportion to your awareness and personal growth.

Beyond recognizing your own role in a conflict, however, and beyond even recognizing who is literally involved in any given conflict, the fundamental component of acceptance goes even deeper. I believe that people are more than the sum of what they've done in life. In other words, I believe that you have an essence that is greater than any individual actions you've ever done. Yes, people see your actions, not your intentions. Yes, people judge you by your actions, whereas they judge themselves in the context of their intentions. We all do. But just as you are more than your actions, I believe everyone else is as well. This fundamental belief that people are more than the sum of their actions is a key part of why Yield Theory is so successful. I confront conflict directly, but I'm mindful to let people know that I see they are more than who they are in their worst moments.

I was in one of Georgia's toughest maximum-security prisons when an inmate was stabbed in another part of the prison. Shortly after, I talked to one of the men who was allegedly involved. The man was irate before I even got to the door of his cell in the restricted housing unit (the "hole"). He was yelling that he was being falsely accused, and he was threatening to assault staff. I listened to what he was saying, and I imagined myself in his shoes as I validated him. He calmed down more quickly than the people observing expected. He eventually said, "You know, you're a very encouraging individual, and if you met me under different circumstances, you'd see that I'm not like this." I looked him in the eyes and said, "I know I might not know you, but one thing I do know about you is that this isn't you. I know you've lived a whole life before this moment, so please don't think for one second that I believe you expressing anger over this situation defines you in any way." Not only did this man calm down completely after that and not act out during my time with him, but when I visited the same prison four months later, the staff reported to me that the man had not acted out at all since that incident.

Specializing in working with people convicted of violent crimes has led to me witnessing or hearing about some of the worst instances of the way humans treat one another. Still, I firmly believe that we are all more than the sum of our actions. And you don't have to enter the "hole" in prison to see that people's expression of anger is not a complete definition of who they are. In Yield Theory, accepting who is involved in conflict means understanding that you are not just talking to the angry person in the moment—you are talking to the entirety of who that person is. Imagine, after all, if you were defined and treated according to your worst, most reckless, impulsive moment. Just like you, people are more than what they do, and the more you are able to convey that even in the heat of conflict, the more validated others will feel. Accepting the deeper view of who is involved helps you approach situations from a broad perspective, and expressing that belief to others can be a shield for you as you walk directly through any anger you encounter.

Accepting Where People Are

▶ In the distant future on a dystopian planet there were no trees or vegetation of any kind, only modern technology. Somehow, some way, however, one day a watermelon sprouted out of a crack in the grand floor. This civilization that was advanced in every way saw the watermelon as a threat. "What could it be?" they wondered. And as suspicions tend to get the best of people, eventually they deemed the watermelon a "monster" and feared it.

A stranger found his way into this technology world, and he insisted on seeing the monster they all feared. The moment he saw it, he recognized it from his travels, and he said immediately and condescendingly, "That's not a monster! It's a watermelon!" He smashed it in half and began to eat it. The people turned pale as ghosts when they saw him do this; by his killing the monster and eating it, they figured, this man must be a monster worse than the first. The angry mob wanted no part of him, so they drove him away.

At about the same time the following year, another watermelon sprouted, and again the people were afraid. Again, too, a stranger was passing through. This stranger, like the first, also immediately recognized the watermelon for what it was, but unlike the first stranger, he also saw how afraid the people were, and so he acted startled to see the watermelon. This second stranger stayed with the people, listened to them, and validated their fears. Every day, he would walk closer to the watermelon and then run away from it. After exploring some different options, he invited others to move closer to it with him, and then, with them at his side, he even reached down and touched it. As he did, they did. Eventually, he was able to show them how to eat it and even cultivate more watermelons. He was a hero for introducing nature into their otherwise stale world, but they forever knew him as the Great Watermelon Slayer. ◀

The story of the Great Watermelon Slayer encapsulates meeting people where they are, not where you think they should be. The first stranger believed the people *should* have known that the watermelon was harmless, and he treated them accordingly. The Great Watermelon Slayer, however, wisely understood the reality that, despite his knowing that it was only a watermelon, the people of that land simply did not have that information. Instead of demanding (even in his own mind) that the people should have been somewhere else in their understanding, he took the time to meet them where they actually were, connect with them, and join with them. He listened, validated, and explored options regarding verifiable facts from another side of the box they could not initially see (that is, watermelons are indeed edible, and they are incapable of attacking).

Accepting where people are does not mean resigning yourself to believing they will always be there. Instead, it identifies a clear starting point from which you can assess their understanding of where they are, as well as assess their readiness and preparedness to get to a different place. Think again of your daughter broken down on the side of the road. To accept the reality of her location isn't to throw your hands up and say, "Oh, well, I guess I'll never see her then." Rather, accepting the reality of where she is allows you to leave where you are and go meet her exactly where she is.

In the early 1980s, two professors from the University of Rhode Island developed one of the most effective tools there is for understanding where people are in regard to their readiness and willingness to change. James Prochaska and Carlo DiClemente called their wonderfully pragmatic model "the stages of change." Although they wrote about six stages, the first four apply most aptly to Yield Theory.

STAGE ONE **Not even thinking about change.** Imagine Rob, a man who's angry and doesn't realize how much his anger affects everyone around him. Maybe someone in his life comes up to him and tells him outright that he needs to get help for his anger. If Rob was in the first stage of change, he would ask that person, "Why?" Oftentimes, when people come to me asking if I think they have a problem with anger, I ask them who's told them that they do. My advice is usually: "If one person has told you something one time in an emotional state, then it might not be true. But if the same person has told you multiple times or, worse, if multiple people have told you the same thing, then it's likely true, and you just can't see it." In the first stage, Rob wouldn't realize he had a problem with anger, and even if it was pointed out to him, he wouldn't really believe it was something he needed to work on changing.

STAGE TWO **Thinking about change but not yet ready to do anything about it.** So let's say I give that advice about multiple people saying something to Rob, and he replies, "Oh, then yes, I probably have an anger problem, because everyone in my life says I do. Okay, I can see that. I guess I should do something about it." Rob's "guessing that he should do something about it" is not a great indicator that he's ready to actually change; but in this second stage, he is at least aware of the issue, which is further along than he was in stage one. If I'm performing an accurate assessment, I would recognize that in this stage, although he might be aware of what he needs to do, he's not yet ready to do it.

STAGE THREE **Making small changes.** In the third stage, Rob is not only aware that he struggles with anger, but he's also ready and prepared to begin working on his impulse control issues. He wouldn't just have awareness in this stage, he would also be working on making the changes he needed to make. The realistic problem to consider is this: Usually by the third stage, people tend to convince themselves that they are actually changing, when in fact they are more likely only taking small steps. Again, remember that people judge themselves by their intentions, not by their actions, so they see even the small changes they're making in light of the big intentions they have. In one sense, this third stage can be seen as extraordinarily empowering, because people are finally doing something about whatever it is that they need to change; but in another sense, people in this stage often see their shifts as more monumental than those on the outside do.

STAGE FOUR **Actually changing.** In the fourth stage, Rob would have gained control over his anger. Time and situations would have demonstrated that he can maintain self-control in conflicts that would previously have set him off. In the fourth stage, people are solidly making the changes that they need to make.

The key to utilizing the stages of change is to help people in one stage gain awareness about where they are and what the next stage is. Your goal is not to move people from stage one to stage four in one fell swoop. So, for instance, if you meet someone where they are in the first stage, then your focus is best spent on helping that person gain awareness about the second stage, not talking to that person as though he or she "should" be in the third or fourth stage. Without awareness of the stages of change, you are likely to talk *at* others instead of *with* them. To me, the definition of nagging is talking to someone who is in stage one as though he or she "should" be in stage four. Work on increasing your awareness of where others are, and put the onus on yourself to meet those people where they actually are rather than trying to force them to be where you think they should be.

When you're assessing your own stage of change in connection with how you handle anger and conflict, it's wise to be easy on yourself and just accurately identify where you are. Wherever you are, the next best step is to move yourself into the next stage, not to try to leap forward by two or three stages at once. Change is a process, and it takes time. The more you learn to accept yourself for where you are, the easier it will be for you to accept others for where they are as well.

Summary

The word "acceptance" can seem misleading in the context of a discussion about anger and conflict, especially if someone assumes that it refers to accepting violence or mistreatment in any way; of course, it does not. The fundamental component of acceptance centers on meeting others where they are and accepting the reality of what is actually happening, who is involved (including you), and, perhaps most importantly, where people are in their readiness and preparedness to change. The goal is for you to employ the kind of self-discipline that allows you to leave where you are to go meet others where they are, not expecting them to know what you know or do what you do, and then help them take the most effective next steps for them, without irrationally demanding that they should magically skip forward to where you want them to be. As you practice recognizing what is actually happening, you can begin to make whatever realistic changes are possible.

Authenticity

Operating from Essence

When people sense that you genuinely care about them and their well-being, aren't judging them, and truly have their best interests in mind, they are incredibly open to hearing anything you have to say, even in the heat of conflict. Since your body language speaks volumes, you cannot fake authenticity. People can spot inauthenticity in you just as easily as you can identify it in them, so if you feign that you care, that you aren't judging, or that you really have others' best interests in mind, you will only contribute to defensiveness, not get through it. In this chapter, I'll show you why it's important to be authentic and how you can listen, validate, and explore options in the most genuine way possible.

The reason the old colloquial phrase "You can't BS a BSer" rings true is that people who practice being deceitful have a more keenly developed ability than the rest of us to pick up on even the most nuanced hints of deceit in others. And it's not magic or a con that makes that happen—it's actually neuroscience, and it's practice. Your brain comes equipped with *mirror neurons*, or neurons that fire in patterns that mentally replicate what you're watching. Mirror neurons are at the root of empathy and vicarious learning. They are, for instance, the reason I teach young athletes to watch the best in their sport perform: As they observe seasoned experts demonstrate the craft, their own brains are replicating the performance. It's "Monkey see, monkey do," except it's quite literally "Person see, person do." We learn first by watching. Of course, when it comes to mastering a skill, watching isn't enough, which is why practicing matters so much. When you recall the idea that we master whatever we practice, it makes a lot of sense that someone who practices deceit (a BSer) gets better at it and that their mirror neurons can be quick to pick up on the deceit (BS) in others.

You don't have to practice deceit to be effective at detecting inauthenticity in others, however, because your own mirror neurons are helping you evaluate every action you see, including micro–facial expressions. And the more you practice intentionally assessing authenticity, the better you get at it. Deceit isn't just about being willfully dishonest or malicious, either; sometimes the defense mechanisms that protect your ego are triggered in ways that can lead to you deceiving yourself. For example, you might be in denial and not consciously realize the discrepancy between what you say and what you do, but other people who are watching you might be able to see that discrepancy pretty easily. Being authentic, then, involves you understanding how your ego can inhibit you from being true to your core, or what I refer to as your *essence*.

Ego is the great instigator and perpetrator of anger and conflict. The need to be right, to get credit for what you do, to be seen in a particular light, or to have things go the way you think they should (in other words, according to your cartoon world) are all centered in ego. When you set your ego aside, you can operate with humility and circumvent others' egos as well, but setting your ego aside and operating from your essence can be very difficult until you understand exactly what that entails.

Ego and Essence

A seed doesn't need to be taught how to grow. Wild animals don't need to be taught how to trust their instincts. Like a seed, you have an innate drive to grow; like all other animals, your instincts come naturally. Consciousness separates you from the majority of other life on this planet; it's a gift that helps you think about thinking, create, communicate complex information in multiple modalities, learn and share ideas from and with those you never have encountered or never will encounter, and pursue self-actualization. Although consciousness gives us the ability to describe our world, it is in and of itself indescribably incredible. Consciousness is not necessary for all life to survive, but it's certainly inescapable for us, and it sure seems to make our lives more beautiful at times. Of course, along with the beauty of consciousness come other, less desirable aspects, such as unnecessary anger, conflict, and unintentional miscommunications.

So perhaps seeds don't create unnecessary suffering for themselves and animals aren't passing down written descriptions of their knowledge for future generations, but we can all learn an awful lot about our essence from observing nature. One of my favorite stories from the Buddha's teachings, in fact, is the legend in which he helped others get to the heart of authenticity by observing nature in the most direct way possible.

▶ Once a large crowd of monks gathered to hear the Buddha speak. They were anxious and excited to hear what the great master might say, but it's said that he stood before them for many minutes without saying a word. He stood in silence, almost statuesque, exuding love and compassion; and then, finally, he held up a single flower for all to see. Without uttering a sound, he looked around and saw that only one among them understood. The Buddha smiled at that monk, realizing that he alone got the lesson. He turned and left, never speaking a word. ◀

That lone monk understood that the flower didn't have to try to be, it just was. It didn't have to talk about its nature to be its nature. You are not a flower, however, and as an inescapably conscious being, consciousness is in your nature. It's not wrong or bad, it just is. The goal is not to shed consciousness or to deny it but to expand it to understand how you can fulfill your potential and perhaps even most effectively *be* in the world. Your psyche is more complex than a flower's, and it's centered in either your ego or its actual center: your essence.

Authenticity requires you to be true to your essence (also referred to as "your authentic self" or "the core of your being"), not your ego. Whereas your ego can be defined as the center of who you convince yourself you are, your essence is the center of your entire being. When Lao Tzu said, "If you try to define yourself, you cannot know who you really are," he was talking about this difference between ego and essence. Karen Horney defined essence as "the alive, unique personal center of ourselves; the only part that can, and wants to, grow." What I love about her definition is that it emphasizes growth. I believe that we are designed to constantly strive. There is a big difference between saying, "I am not enough" and saying, "There is always more to learn." Like the flower, you are enough exactly as you are; but as long as you are alive, there is always room for you to grow. Just as we need to take in food every day, regardless of how full we might have been yesterday, I believe we can constantly feed the core of who we are with knowledge and self-discovery. The key to learning about yourself starts with understanding the difference between your ego and your essence. In 1915, Sigmund Freud came up with a great model for explaining the psyche, which holds both.

Think of your psyche as an iceberg. The center of the part that rises above water is your ego; the center of the whole iceberg, however, is your essence. Your ego is vastly more exposed than the core of your being, and the ego is the center of your conscious awareness. It's important to you because it's the part you genuinely see, so your psyche works to protect it. Your ego uses defense mechanisms to guard its sense of certainty. Just as it's easier to stand on the small exposed part of the iceberg than on its deeper core, which is steeped in the dark depths, it's likewise easier to live from a place of ego—so we do. It's easier, for instance, to convince yourself that whatever you think and believe about the world is correct and any thoughts that oppose your views are incorrect. This sense of certainty leads us to exude the kind of arrogance that perpetuates disagreements; it keeps us viewing conflict as a contest (my ego versus your ego), which naturally results in a one-up and one-down, winner and loser paradigm. Even when people agree to disagree, each still believes that they are right and that the other person is wrong.

Where your essence is open to learning and wants to grow, your ego is locked into certainty and rigidity, but for a good reason. Evolution has been helpful to our cognitive development, and the more we've been able to learn, the better we've been able to survive. On the most primal level, not knowing what's around the corner can produce physiological fear, because whatever's around the corner could lead to our death (a poisonous snake, a bear, or any other wild animal potentially spelled doom to our ancient ancestors). Although our modern perspective of the world and the universe might be more expansive than the view from a cave and the surrounding area, or even the miles of ground our nomadic ancestors covered in their travels, the reality is that not knowing what's around the corner is still scary—especially if that corner is the edge of the ego's belief system. Think, after all, about how big the universe is. We live in a solar system with more or fewer planets than you might have grown up learning we have (depending on your definition of "planet"), in a galaxy with hundreds of billions of stars, in a universe that consists of an estimated two trillion galaxies to date and (if string theory ends up having any merit) a potentially unlimited number of universes or multiverses. In a space that astronomically extensive, certainty is more recognizable as a feeling than as an objective fact, but it's something that our egos cling to nonetheless.

Robert A. Burton, a neuroscientist who has studied certainty for the majority of his thirty-year career, has found that the feeling of certainty arises in different brain regions from those associated with thinking. Moreover, he has found that conflict between logic and a feeling of knowing tends to be resolved in favor of feeling. That is why opposing groups of people are so adamant that their vastly different conclusions are certain. One group, for instance, proclaims, "There is a God!" and another group proclaims, "No, there's no such thing as God!" And regardless of the absence of irrefutable proof, both groups are certain they're correct, and anger ensues.

Ultimately, when egos collide, conflict arises. Two egos, each protected by multiple defense mechanisms, are like two armies facing off against each other. When they stand toe to toe, the potential for

conflict escalates. The following story illustrates what two egos collid-
ing looks like, as well as what it looks like when you can move past
others' defense mechanisms.

▶ Two kings were about to go to war when one of them realized that it
was unnecessary for thousands of soldiers to die simply because the
two kings had a disagreement. He said that he would travel straight
through the other king's army to speak directly to him. Legend has
it that his mission to do such a noble deed impressed the gods, and
they sent a magical being to hand the compassionate king an amulet
of invincibility to help him in his quest.

The king put the amulet on and then walked through the other army.
The fearful enemy king had his army fire shot after shot at the compassionate king; the soldiers swung swords at his head and tried to stab
him with spears, but all to no avail. The amulet of invincibility kept this
kind king safe, and he made it all the way to the enemy king's chambers.

The moment he arrived in front of his opponent, the other king,
shocked from having watched the compassionate king walk through
his army unscathed, apologized profoundly for having his soldiers
attack him and asked what he could do to bring about peace. The
compassionate king accepted his apology, and the two of them sat
down to work out their differences. ◀

The compassionate king represents essence, or the authentic self. The
fearful enemy represents ego. The soldiers are the defense mechanisms.
The amulet of invincibility is the knowledge that your essence cannot
be harmed by others' defense mechanisms, because your essence
understands that defense mechanisms are illusions designed to keep
egos safe. When you avoid engaging in fighting others' defense mechanisms, you can move past them to their authentic core. Circumventing
others' defense mechanisms does not mean skirting around an issue or
not directly confronting others. Instead, it involves you taking a direct
path to the essence of others by wearing your own "amulet of invincibility" and not taking others' pain personally. When you connect your
essence with the core of others, you're on a path of striking together
with them, rather than *at* them.

It's crucial to understand the difference between ego and essence, because without understanding that difference, you might refer to yourself as being "authentic" or "real" simply because you are willing to speak whatever impulsive thoughts arise in your mind, without evaluating the readiness or willingness of others to listen to what you have to say. Doing things like "just speaking your mind" or "saying what you really feel" or even "telling others how it is" arises from ego. When you speak assertively from your ego, you make the issue about you being right or maybe even about you saving others and being the hero. Speaking assertively from your essence, however, allows you to lead with humility and compassion as you directly confront others in a way that assesses their stage of change and helps you speak in ways that can actually be heard.

Moving beyond your ego and getting closer to your authentic core takes effort. Just as it's more difficult to dive down into the dark depths to find the center of an iceberg, it's more difficult to operate from your essence than to stay in your ego. The more true you are to your core, though, the easier it is to be genuinely open and humble (because it's a state of constant awareness and growth), which immediately puts you in a better position to lessen conflict. From your authentic core, you will recognize that you're limited to seeing your side of the box, that you truly don't have all the answers, and that others' perceptions and experiences are as valid as your own. Whereas the ego is insecure, fearful, and convinced that it's right, the essence is curious and interested in learning about others' perspectives. When you come from a place of authentic compassion, humility, and genuine care and concern for others, you will find that people are often willing to drop their defenses and accept direct feedback; and even if they fire the best of their defenses at you, you will avoid taking this personally.

Authenticity, then, entails humility. Few people feel threatened when they encounter a humble personality. In a time of conflict—when so many people are led by their egos convincing them that their perspectives are the correct ones and that those who think, feel, believe, or behave differently are wrong—being humble is not only refreshing, it's the key to communicating effectively. Think about your own experiences, for example: In times when you've been angry, would you rather have encountered a self-absorbed, egotistical know-it-all or one who was humbly open to learning your perspective and genuinely invested in wanting to help? Being humble does not mean you have to eschew strength or assertiveness or even give up believing what's important to you, but it does involve being open to learning constantly. To paraphrase Mark Twain: Speak with conviction, but be open to being wrong. In other words, you might feel comfortable about what you know and believe in the current moment, but you can also be open to new information and what you might learn in the next. This attitude of being a constant learner sets you up to listen, validate, and explore options in ways that others will be amenable to accepting.

Listen with Authenticity

There's a great anecdote about a little girl who comes into the kitchen while her mother is cleaning up. The little girl starts to tell her mother a story that includes the tiniest details about a make-believe game she's playing with her toys, when all of a sudden she stops and says, "Listen, Mommy!" To which her mother responds defensively, "I am listening." And the little girl replies, "Yes, but I mean listen with your eyes."

You know when people are giving you their full attention, and they know when you are as well. Although the ego might try to convince us that we can give our full attention to multiple tasks at one time, modern neuroscience demonstrates that multitasking is a myth: The scientific evidence points to the phenomenon that people refer to as "multitasking" as the brain simply shifting focus rapidly back and forth between two or among multiple tasks. So whereas your ego might defensively proclaim, "I am listening!" when told otherwise, your authentic core might say, "I'm so sorry. You're right. I was distracted." So be genuine about whether you can listen in the moment, and then be mindful to exhibit the behaviors that show your focus is where you say it is. Walking through anger and handling conflict is not about your ego being right, it's about connecting with others, circumventing their defensiveness, and communicating in ways that are heard. All this begins with being authentic as you listen. Any time you spend defending what you were doing is time focused on your side of the box; the actual act of listening occurs most effectively when it centers on others, not you.

Listening from your authentic essence is marked by genuine curiosity to hear what others are expressing about their experience from their side of the box. The fastest way to check whether you're listening with your ego or with your essence lies in your judgment. If you believe, for example, that what others are saying is "stupid," then your judgment indicates that you're listening from ego. When you listen with humble curiosity to learn what others are seeing on their side of the box, however, you're listening from your essence. Judgments arise from your ego's need to confirm what it "knows" about its world; hence, judgments impede growth. The more you judge, the more you stay locked in your ego and its limited perspective. This doesn't mean that you can't have judgments or that you should pretend that you don't. Rather, the goal is to shine light on the judgments you do have and humbly recognize that you, like me and everyone else, are also in the labyrinth at times. It's one thing to give lip service to the phrase "I still have more to learn," and it's another thing altogether to live that message out.

There are other ways in which we listen from our ego and impede our authenticity. *Confirmation bias* is the concept that we have a tendency to see whatever it is that we're looking to see. In other words, if you want to see someone as "bad," it doesn't matter how many good things that person does—you will wait for, highlight, and amplify whatever that person does that you perceive to be "bad." Whatever your ego already believes, it seeks out new information to confirm. It is psychologically easier on your ego to believe that you are already right and that you just need evidence to confirm what you already know rather than for your ego to face the vast immensity of knowledge that sits outside of its domain.

Perhaps one of the clearest examples of confirmation bias inhibiting people from listening authentically in our modern, emotionally charged world comes from observing the interaction of two political pundits with opposing views. Although people who hold extreme views are on both sides of the proverbial political fence, those with a strong political bent to one side will likely pay attention only to the ridiculous and outlandish things that are said and done by those on the side they disagree with, and then they'll likely either highlight or run with those ideas. Even beyond politics, people with a strong attachment to a particular group will rely on the ego defense mechanism of confirmation bias to reassure themselves that however they see the world is the "correct" way to see it. And, of course, members of each group will spot the confirmation bias in the other group while minimizing their own use of it, because it's much easier to identify that bias in others than it is to accept it in ourselves.

You use confirmation bias. Those who think differently from you use it. I do. We all do. We look for evidence to confirm what we already believe, because having to constantly challenge our own belief system is scary. In fact, it's far too scary to earnestly entertain; that is, until we are serious about being ready to challenge what we know and believe and when we're actually ready to walk through anger. Once we're serious enough about our own personal growth, we can begin to be aware of our confirmation bias, and we can even begin to lessen it (although I would argue philosophically that it might not be possible to eliminate entirely). The more comfortable you can become in not having answers, the more open you'll be to challenging your own confirmation biases. Challenging your confirmation biases is imperative before you can set your ego aside and be genuine as you listen.

Authenticity in Validation

The more you seek to see the world from other people's perspectives, the easier it becomes to set your ego aside. Remember that validation doesn't require you to condone what others do, only to acknowledge what they're communicating, their state of mind, or their perception of what they're experiencing. Although people can tell if you're being insincere, they can also sense when you provide genuine, heartfelt validations, and the more sincere you are in acknowledging what others are experiencing, the faster you can move through the intense emotions and work toward solutions. Being kind to someone by genuinely acknowledging their pain, even if they are the cause of their own pain and "shouldn't have done" whatever they did in the first place, is transformative. It's healing.

Validation connects us with others in powerful ways. Authentic validation involves acknowledging (even internally) the inherent limitations of our understanding. The fact is that we all have our own subjective, phenomenological experience of life that others cannot see, and your acknowledging that unseeable aspect can feel extremely validating for others to hear. When people are hurting and angry, they're often quick to tell you that you "don't" or "can't" understand. When people tell you that you "couldn't possibly understand" what they're going through, your ego will demand that you show them that they're wrong, that you do understand, and your mind will race with logical answers that prove you're right. The process looks something like this.

> **Angry person:** "You don't know what it's like to be me! You can't understand what I'm going through!"

> **Ego:** "Yes, I do. I've been where you are. I know exactly what you're going through!"

Your essence, on the other hand, will comfortably accept its limitations and then be content with validating the isolated feeling it hears others expressing. That process looks like this.

> **Angry person:** "You don't know what it's like to be me! You can't understand what I'm going through!"

> **Essence:** "You're right. I can't. But I'm here with you, and I'm willing to learn."

Being authentic as you validate is like being willing to run a race you will never finish, but being willing to put forth the effort as though you will. You have to be prepared to participate and give your all to the race, especially knowing that there is no end to it. That's a difficult concept for a lot of people, but it is the heart of expressing validation authentically in Yield Theory, and it is the embodiment of seeing conflict as an opportunity to strike together with the other person rather than as a contest or competition. People's psychological experience of life is entirely unique to them, as yours is to you. Total understanding is neither possible nor the goal of connecting through validation. Authentic validation is centered in *trying* to understand while being willing to let go of the need to proclaim that you *do* entirely understand.

Ultimately, to embrace the uniqueness of others' individual psyches is to acknowledge the ineffable depth of your own psyche. You never have to have had others' experience of life to validate the experience, ideas, or emotions they're communicating. Even identical twins in exactly the same situations have their own unique and nuanced experiences of those situations, and neither can entirely understand the other's experience. The more you want to understand what others are experiencing and are simultaneously willing to let go of proclaiming (even to yourself) that you completely understand, the faster you'll be able to connect with others. When you reflect what you hear from your essence, you bypass others' egos as well. Validation in this way is the core of genuine connection.

Exploring Options with Authenticity

Exploring options might seem like the easiest thing to do authentically. After all, in many situations, a limited number of behavioral choices exist. For example, in every conflict, people can do one of four things: (1) say something, (2) say nothing, (3) do something, or (4) do nothing. That's it. Once you understand that behavioral reality, helping others come to that realization too is a pretty black and white matter. Now, what people say and how they say it are wide open and where all the gray exists, and the same is true for what they do and how they do it; but, ultimately, there really are only four overarching behavioral choices in every situation. So what does it mean to be authentic in exploring options?

It means identifying the realistic options that exist, which begins with acknowledging the options people are considering first. It doesn't matter if what others are considering is awful and something that you don't want them to choose, because as long as they're only considering it and not doing it, nothing bad is happening. Being authentic means acknowledging that every viable choice a person considers is a reality. Telling people that they cannot do something you don't want them to do is not only unrealistic, but I would argue that it also strengthens their consideration of that option.

Remember, our egos want to prove themselves right, and that's especially true of an angry, impulsive ego, so telling an angry ego that it can't do something is likely to exacerbate its willingness to prove you wrong. Whatever option someone's considering *is* an option, but that doesn't mean it's the *only* option. The good news is that even though the ego is rigid, essence is constantly striving to learn, so responding to others from your essence and connecting with their essence allows you to guide them to becoming open to alternate options.

By not resisting others as they articulate their first viable option, you take away their ego's desire to defend what they can and can't do, and the less defensive they are, the more open they'll be to exploring other options. Natural consequences are inevitable. In other words, if you're angry and you punch a brick wall, you're likely going to hurt your hand. Can you punch the wall? Yes. Do you feel like punching the wall? Yes. Are there going to be immediate, painful natural consequences (for example, breaking your hand) if you punch the wall? Yes. So it's true that punching the wall is an option. And it certainly makes sense why, if you were filled with negative energy, you might want to release that energy pretty quickly, so I can understand your reason for wanting to punch the wall. This makes it easy for me to validate anyone who really does want to hit a wall. But—and this is important—it's also easy for me to explore the very real and painful consequences that you would likely have from hitting the wall.

Ego is set on finding a quick fix or immediate pleasure; but essence is patient and mindful of the big picture. Exploring options from your authentic self helps you keep the big picture in mind. Moments of anger—and all emotions, actually—are fleeting. Actions, on the other hand, are permanent. The ego tends to make decisions to satiate immediate feelings, whereas essence tends to consider the long-term consequences that might result from the immediate actions. The more you operate from your essence, the more calm and centered you'll be, and the more likely you are to elicit the essence of others.

There's a difference between teaching others by shining light on areas that were otherwise unseen and trying to control. Our authentic essence is humble, and it respects others' choices. That is why Lao Tzu says in the Tao Te Ching, "In governing, don't try to control." As you will see with the fundamental component of nonattachment, being unbiased by personal interest and not influenced by selfish motives is in line with truly respecting others' freedom. Although your ego (via your cartoon world) might try to convince you that you know what's best for others, or your ego might want others to make decisions that somehow credit you, your essence respects that there are always factors you simply cannot see. A good strategy for helping people steer themselves down more effective paths is to assist them in uncovering the wisdom they already have within. Again, from Lao Tzu, he asks, "Can you love the people and lead them, without imposing your will?" The less you try to determine the outcome for others, the more you can compassionately observe the path that others take. Without having to defend or justify their choices to you, people can focus their energy on whether they want to actually make the choices they're considering, including dealing with the consequences of their actions.

Exploring honest options from your authentic self means being mindful that every choice has a consequence, and respecting others' free will to choose is not the same as letting people get away with whatever they want without a consequence. When you explore options from your essence, you can state matter-of-factly what consequences are likely to follow, and that can include setting very clear boundaries for yourself. In other words, you can respect where a person is coming from but still set whatever parameters are necessary to set. In fact, even in some of the toughest environments possible (such as maximum-security prisons), the more clearly the boundaries are set and subsequent consequences stated, the less likely people are to cross those boundaries.

▶ A worm befriended a toad, and the two of them played on land for a time, but soon the toad wanted to swim in the water. The worm, insecure about her inability to join her friend and swim, became angry at the toad. The worm called the toad many names, until finally the toad placed his webbed feet firmly in the mud and said, "You may call me any names you wish, but I am going in the water nonetheless.

What I can tell you is this: If you choose to call me one more name, I will never come back to this side of the pond again." And the worm apologized quickly, realizing that if she did not, she would lose her friend for good. ◀

When you are clear in exploring options and their inevitable outcomes, you can be unattached to the result. Being kind and compassionate and setting judgments aside can go hand in hand with setting firm boundaries to avoid being walked over.

Living Authenticity

Your personal growth is integral to how you handle conflict. It's important to remember that no matter how much thought you might be putting into your internal development, people can see only what you do, not what you mean or don't mean to do. What you think contributes to how you act, though, and from your mannerisms to your facial expressions to your posture to the way you move, your presence precedes you. When you become aware of your presence, you can intentionally shape it.

An ineluctable reality is this: You are always emitting energy. The energy you bring to situations affects them. If you authentically exude interest, compassion, respect, patience, and peace, you'll be able to handle any conflict effectively. To live that way takes ongoing effort—that is, until it doesn't. In other words, it takes effort to learn about yourself and why you do the things you do, but once you really understand you (your essence), moving through your emotional states becomes a seamless process.

The more true you are to your essence (that innately humble and curious part of you that always wants to grow), the easier it will be for others to pick up on your authenticity. Knowing yourself and understanding the energy you give off will undoubtedly lead to more consistency between what you say and how you say it.

It's great, for instance, to say the phrase "Stay humble," but what does that really mean? Or—more relevant to your own life—how can you actually practice being humble? The answer lies in deepening your understanding of ego and essence, including just how hard ego works to maintain the illusion that the answers and beliefs you have about life are the correct perspectives. As you have seen, ego is central to conflict and anger, so continually chipping away at understanding the defense mechanisms that lock you into your ego is crucial to breaking free from it. In addition to the confirmation bias that keeps you in psychological blinders, causing you to see only what your ego wants to see, there are other defense mechanisms that trap you in the arrogance of ego. One such defense mechanism is *hindsight bias*.

▶ A town operated its entire way of life from a giant piece of machinery. When that machine broke, the townspeople were up in arms. They tried everything they knew to fix this machine, but nothing they did worked. Finally they called in an expert. The expert said he could fix the machine, so the townspeople felt a sense of great hope.

When the expert said his fee would be twenty million dollars, the townspeople didn't hesitate to agree to it. "We cannot get this machine to work, so even though your price is extremely high, we realize that we cannot function without our machine. Our entire way of life is dependent on it." The expert demanded to be paid up front, and when the check had cleared, he walked down to the basement where the machine was located, and he pulled out a tiny hammer the size of a pinky finger. He located a very specific spot on the machine, and he tapped ever so lightly three times with his tiny hammer.

The machine kicked back on, and the people cheered. But then it hit them that all this man had done was tap lightly three times on one spot. They became outraged that they had paid a ridiculously high price for this simple task. "That's not fair!" they cried. "All you did was tap three times with your stupid tiny little hammer!" And more anger ensued.

When everyone quieted down, the expert said, "Yes, but I knew where to tap." ◀

Of course, once people see the answer, they no longer remember that moments prior they did not have the answer and could not solve the problem. The ego convinces us that we actually knew the answer all along, when in fact we didn't. That is hindsight bias, and it comes from an egoic position of arrogance. Like confirmation bias, hindsight bias plays a central role in blocking authenticity. Think about a past encounter with a brain teaser that stumped you. The moment you got the answer, your ego raced to convince you that you actually had that answer all along and that "I was going to say that!" You weren't. If you had had the answer, you would have said it.

Hindsight bias is significant when it comes to anger and communication and authenticity, because without an awareness that we're engaging in it, we can come across as arrogant know-it-alls. As you know from encountering know-it-alls in your own life, they evoke more defensiveness than openness, as their insecurities can trigger your own insecurities. If we're not secure with ourselves and we interact with someone who tells us they have all the answers, the first thing we do is seek to prove that person wrong. Anchored in unconscious insecurities, confirmation bias drives us to prove others wrong, and hindsight bias drives us to prove ourselves right.

Now think about this in terms of trying to approach others in conflict, or walking through anger. If hindsight bias drives you to approach others as if you believe you have all the answers, you will likely add to their defensiveness, not help them move through it. In a sense, hindsight bias is you telling others that you already saw the side of the box that they uniquely see. Understanding both hindsight and confirmation bias is crucial, because once we understand that there are tremendous limitations to what we can know and what we seek to know, then we are able to approach others in a humble way. When you approach others with humility, they are much less likely to be defensive.

Hindsight bias also shapes the way we see anger, conflict, and behavior. For example, before a person engages in any action, it's easy to subscribe to the idea that people do the best they can with what they have in any given moment. But the minute the person takes an action and the results are clear, it's much easier to jump to the conclusion that the person knew better, but just didn't care. Again, your ego's natural tendency is to gloat in certainty. If, however, you continue to embrace the philosophy that people do the best they can even after you know the result of their actions, it will make sense to you to meet people where they are, so that you can teach them from there (rather than assuming, from your cartoon world perspective, that they "should have known better").

Our authentic selves are secure and humble; they are okay with not having all the answers. That is why Lao Tzu advised, "The master leads by emptying people's minds and filling their cores." The goal with the fundamental component of authenticity in Yield Theory is to lead, not with certainty, but with humility and inquisitiveness, and to invite humility in return. Stepping out of the cultural pressures and concepts that convince us our way is right and others who think, feel, believe, or behave differently are wrong sets us up to exude a safe energy to be around. Approaching others with authenticity matters.

Understanding the limits of human thinking is central to living authentically. If your essence wants to grow, then the less certain (and more curious) you are, the more humble you will be. Humility is the key to walking straight through anger. The vast majority of anger stems from attachment to certainty (people thinking, "Things should be this way!" or "Things shouldn't be this way!" or "You must see things my way!"). The arrogance of certainty sets up and perpetuates conflict, so being able to approach others in conflict from a place of humility and curiosity is a profound tack to take, and it radically shifts the energy of anger.

Summary

Be yourself. Be true to who you really are, though, not just true to your ego. Your ego will try to convince you that being right is a position of power or that you need others to see what you see, but the reality is that your authentic self is much deeper than your ego, and your authentic self is curious and open to learning. To exude authenticity the next time you're in a conflict, do your best to approach others with a genuine interest in learning about their side of the box and with a humility that shows, by your actions, that you're not convinced you have all the answers. People can tell when you're authentic. When you can operate from your essence, you increase your chances of circumventing others' defensiveness and connecting with them in genuine ways.

> Anger will never be overcome by anger,
> but by love alone.
> **THE BUDDHA**

Compassion

Overcoming Anger

If you approach anger with anger, as the Buddha taught more than two millennia ago, you will only add to conflict, not lessen it. It's easy to respond to your own anger impulsively, and it's even easier to judge others for the impulsive reactions that stem from their anger. It can be tough to have compassion for people who have just acted or reacted out of anger, because anger and its manifestations can certainly be scary. Regardless of how difficult it might be to practice, however, the reality is that, objectively, the Buddha was right: Compassion is what transforms anger. In fact, when you truly exude compassion for yourself and others, your energy is peaceful, your self-talk is balanced, and your presence is safe for others to be around. Your ability to circumvent others' fight-or-flight response and effectively handle anger and conflict increases dramatically.

Having control over your energy can be challenging at times, and having control over your energy in the face of anger and conflict can be even more so; that is why I say that Yield Theory is easy to understand but difficult to practice. Knowing about compassion intellectually and even fully buying into it as an effective approach for handling anger are not the same as actually practicing it. In this chapter, I will present a perspective on compassion that you can integrate into your daily life, as well as some hands-on exercises you can do to increase your compassion for others.

Compassion as Perspective

The word "compassion" stems from the Latin *compati*, which means "to suffer with." To show compassion is to demonstrate to others that you are willing to at least see, if not in some way feel, their pain. In other words, when others perceive that you understand the side of the box they're sharing with you, they will likely feel that you get why they did what they did. If you try to imagine yourself as the person you're talking to—complete with their cognitive functioning, affective capabilities, and life experiences—you naturally can share in trying to understand the world from their perspective.

From a standpoint of compassion, "suffering with" someone circumvents the me-versus-you contest narrative of conflict and moves us right into the realm of the striking together definition. As others sense that you are authentically seeking to share the load of what they're experiencing (even by listening as accurately as possible), they will be quick to drop their defenses and let you inside their psychological world—or inside their vehicle, as the original metaphor of Yield Theory offers. From there it is not difficult to influence people to steer themselves down a different path.

There is a reason why people do the things they do. Explaining behavior, of course, is not the same thing as excusing it. I don't condone, justify, or minimize violence; but I can explain it. Sometimes people act in harmful ways because of impulsivity, past experiences, cognitive functioning, selfishness, beliefs, or even reasons not yet fully understood—but there are always precursors to why people lash out and hurt others. Your knowing there's always a reason why people do what they do, even if you cannot immediately identify what that reason is, can profoundly shift your perspective.

Your perspective affects the way you experience the world. If being stuck in traffic is making you late for something important, for instance, and you take the perspective that everything happens for a reason, then you will likely be sitting in gratitude while you wait. If your perspective, however, is driven by your cartoon world ("This traffic jam shouldn't be happening!"), then you will likely sit in impatience and anger. Either way, the traffic around you is the same; your perspective drives how you experience that moment. Your perspective determines how you experience all moments, in fact, and then of course your experiences influence your perspective. When it comes to handling anger and conflict, keeping compassion in the foreground of your perspective and nonjudgmentally seeing people's actions in the context of a bigger picture radically shift the energy you bring to what you encounter.

It's generally easier to see your own actions from the perspective of a bigger picture. You know that in every situation you've ever experienced, there was always more going on in your mind than what people saw. Because you're the only one with complete, unrestricted access to your mind, you're the only one who knows the true extent of the racing thoughts you've had, the internal battles you've fought, or even all the impulsive thoughts that have gone through your mind—including the countless that you've resisted. Some combination of multiple factors have influenced your every move—biological forces like impulse and desire, your sense of curiosity, your selfishness or altruism, your physiological or emotional state, and on and on. But at the end of the day, the world only ever saw your actions, not your intentions or thoughts or the myriad underlying factors that shaped your decisions. As a result, people judged you on your actions alone.

That is why compassion is the foundational perspective of Yield Theory: because there is so much more to your complete human experience than just your observable actions, and I believe that is true not only for you but for everyone else.

When you engage in the exercise of imagining yourself as others entirely, even with their faculties, you avoid the trap of judgmentally proclaiming "what I would do if I were in your shoes." That exercise helps you realize that you being in their shoes is still you being *you*, with your same cognitive functioning, emotional range, and life experiences. Sure, you've had tough times and didn't do X (fill in the X with anything others do that you might judge), but you chose not to do X from *your* neurons firing precisely as they did in those exact moments, not someone else's. No matter how similar your life obstacles appear to be to anyone else's, they were always your obstacles alone, from your unique perception and perspective, just as all other people's obstacles and experiences are theirs alone. The more you strive to understand the great complexity that has led to people's actions, the more you will understand that it is not about who is right and who is wrong or who has done things better or worse, but about how your energy (the only person's energy you can control) can affect the anger and conflict presently at hand.

The way you approach others shifts when you take the perspective that you cannot reasonably say what you would have done differently in their situation. Like the Great Watermelon Slayer, you don't have to demand that others should know what you know or do what you do. As you try to see what others are seeing, you are able to lead with compassion in a way that helps others feel safe enough to drop their defenses, invite you into their phenomenological worlds, and feel as though you are, in whatever way you can be, suffering with them—even if your suffering only involves you validating the pain they are experiencing. Expressing that you get what others are communicating (which is different from expressing that you "completely understand" them) is a powerful way to help people feel comfortable enough to de-escalate around you.

Any interaction you have with others, especially when it comes to anger, is a shared experience. When you're angry with others or they with you, the connection binds you, at least in that emotional experience. Because psychological pain is essentially abstract but can still feel overwhelming, seeing it in terms of metaphors can make it tangible and manageable. For example, imagine that anger is a heavily weighted object that people carry unnecessarily. Seen this way, the concept of compassion as suffering with others doesn't entail you inflicting pain on yourself, but rather lending a hand to help others carry that weight—even momentarily.

Imagine a man trying to carry a huge log by himself. Since the log is heavy and awkward, all of his energy is devoted to trying to hold onto it, and he can't even step back and question if it's worthwhile for him to continue to carry it. When I interact with someone who is struggling with anger, I visualize that I run over to the person and take one end of the piece of wood to significantly lighten their load. Then, with the two of us bearing the psychological weight together, the other person has enough mental space to step back and ask themselves if they truly need to be carrying the log in the first place. When people have the opportunity to reflect, unhindered by having to defend why they're carrying their "anger log" in the first place, they become open to setting it down. In other words, by listening and validating with compassion, I can help people move away from operating out of their more reactive emotional system and begin exploring realistic options from their higher-level decision-making center.

As you embrace compassion as your perspective, you will find that the incredible ability to exude tremendous compassion resides right at your fingertips.

▶ Once there was an envious monk who wanted to get rid of the Buddha. He figured that if he could kill the Buddha, all the monks would follow him instead. So he devised a plan to provoke and release one of the king's giant warrior elephants the next morning at the exact time the Buddha would set out along the streets to beg for alms. His plan was to get the elephant inebriated, poke at it with a spear, and then release it from its chains so the elephant would trample the Buddha to death in what would appear to be an accident.

But one of the Buddha's most faithful monks just happened to overhear the plan and raced to tell the Buddha what he heard. Despite his faithful friend begging him not to go out the following morning, the Buddha simply smiled calmly and said everything would be okay. The next morning, the envious monk went through with his plan, got the elephant inebriated, poked at it with a spear, and released it from its chains. The elephant stomped wildly and recklessly through the streets, and the people were all afraid. At the other end of town, the Buddha started out down the road, insisting all his monks stand behind him.

Sure enough, the elephant came pounding toward the Buddha. The Buddha, however, stood firmly planted in the middle of the road, dug deeply into the endless wellspring of compassion he held within, and sent what was equivalent to oceanic waves of compassion straight toward the stomping, enraged elephant.

The waves of compassion echoed out from the Buddha so strongly and hit the beast so powerfully that the giant creature slowed down from a run to a walk to a stroll. When it was almost stopped about ten yards from the Buddha, the Honored One smiled at the elephant and motioned for it to come forward. The elephant approached the Buddha and bowed at his feet. The Buddha put his hand on the elephant's head and put his forehead lovingly against the animal's.

The people were amazed, and as they talked among themselves in awe, the Buddha slipped off, smiling. It is said that a small boy noticed this, ran to catch up with him, and asked him why he was smiling. The Buddha said, "All these people think that what just happened was a miracle from me, but I am smiling because what I know is that the oceanic wave of compassion I sent to that poor, angry elephant is the same oceanic wave that can be summoned by all people, at any time." And he continued on his way.

The boy caught up to him again at the outskirts of town, and this time he said, "I have to know: Are you a god?" To which the Buddha smiled and replied, "No."

The boy asked, "Are you an angel?" To which the Buddha said, "No."

And the boy asked, "Are you a saint?" The Buddha just smiled kindly and shook his head no.

Finally, the boy asked, "Well, then, what are you?" And the Buddha said, "I am awake." ◀

As long as you participate in life, you are likely to encounter elephant-sized, seemingly unstoppable, raging emotions, either others' or your own. When you do, it's wise to remember that the oceanic waves of compassion the Buddha sent out from his core are in fact the same waves that exist inside of you. When you practice compassion exercises through meditation, you will develop and enhance your ability to send those waves far out in front of you. Even by visualizing exuding compassion, you are amplifying your compassion. And brain scans second that. In states of compassion, you can exude the type of safe energy that others, via their mirror neurons, can pick up on even subconsciously. With practice, you will be able to walk through anger the way the Buddha faced the angry elephant.

How to Increase Your Compassion

You can't hug someone if there are walls between the two of you. It's equally difficult to connect with others when there are too many psychological barriers between you. Although you cannot account for the barriers others put up, you can certainly attempt to clear your own. By working on yourself and clearing the barriers that exist on your end, you make yourself a safe space to be around psychologically. The safer others feel around you, the less need they have to keep their own protective walls up. Removing the walls that protect your ego and place unnecessary obstacles between you and others takes self-awareness and effort, but one of the fastest ways of lowering your walls and making yourself a safe space is directly tied to your ability to exude compassion.

Research has demonstrated that there are hands-on, pragmatic ways for you to increase your sense of compassion. The following two very effective practices stem from Buddhist traditions; however, you do not have to subscribe to any particular theology to practice them.

Compassion Meditation

In the most basic compassion meditation, the goal is to wish health, peace, and good intentions to others, even to those with whom you are very angry. The practice involves saying three basic statements. The technique is to start with yourself, then move to the next closest person to you, and then move out farther and farther until eventually you can say this meditation for those with whom you are angry. The statements are:

- May X be healthy.

- May X be peaceful.

- May all of X's good intentions be fulfilled.

Even the most cynical, selfish person can see value in wishing health, peace, and good intentions to others: A person who is healthy, peaceful, and exuding only good intentions is not likely to cause much strife. But beyond that, the more you practice wishing health, peace, and good intentions to others, the more gray matter increases in the specific brain regions that light up when you exude compassion. In other words, even if you are only "faking it until you make it," you *will* eventually make it.

The reason behind starting with yourself in this meditation is it's generally easier to wish health and peace for yourself, as few wish to be ill or in states of unrest. Then, as you move out in concentric circles, beginning with those whom you care about the most, you are setting a strong foundation from which to build your compassion outward. If at any point you find it difficult to say this meditation for someone, go back to the beginning and start over. Saying it for yourself first is important, as you are the source of your compassion. Be easy on yourself if you just can't muster up the ability to say it for someone with whom you're really struggling. By continuously coming back to the people you *can* do it for, you're building strength in your compassion.

It's common to reach a point in this exercise where you just begin to say it unconsciously for those you struggle with the most. As with all practices, the more you say it, the easier it gets to say it again.

Seven Breaths

Tonglen is a powerfully transformative meditation in which the practitioner visualizes breathing in the pain of others and then exhaling a healing balm back to them. The idea stems from the belief that divinity exists inside all of us and that when we breathe in the pain of others, the pain never actually enters us but rather is transformed before it even reaches us. In essence, we are not taking on the pain of others but siphoning enough of it to rid them of it, returning only healing energy to them.

To the most skeptical among us, this is a silly visualization with no merit. But to the neuroscientist who evaluates brain functioning in the context of what patients report regarding their current cognitions, an exercise like this can shrink the amygdala and lessen the excretion of cortisol, a stress hormone, while increasing the excretion of the bonding hormone oxytocin. In short, that means that you can move from feeling anxious or even angry to feeling loving-kindness.

Loving-kindness is the goal of tonglen. Seven Breaths is a meditation I developed exactly seven years ago; I promised myself I wouldn't publish it until I had practiced it every day for at least seven years. How time flies. Seven Breaths is a tonglen exercise that does not take long to do but can set you up to approach your day from a vastly expanded perspective. The meditation exercise entails starting with yourself and your loved ones and eventually branching out to all dimensions and reality, both known and unknown. I practice this meditation every day, have for seven years, and have watched profound transformations in both me and those around me result from my doing it.

Practicing Seven Breaths is simple but potent. As the name states, you take seven breaths; with each breath, you breathe in the pain and suffering of others and breathe healing energy back out to them. The first tonglen breath you take is for yourself and your family. So you might imagine your ethereal self hovering above your family and you, breathe in and visualize taking in all of your own suffering and pain, and then exhale and visualize sending healing energy back to your family and you. The second breath is for all living beings on the continent where you are: Breathe in their pain and suffering, breathe out healing energy to them. The third breath is for the world and, again, all life in it. The fourth breath is for all life in the galaxy. Think about it: There are more than 100 billion stars in our galaxy, and there is countless potential for life; so you would imagine breathing in the pain of all of that life, and then breathing out healing energy toward all of it. The fifth breath you take is for the surrounding galaxies; again, visualize all of the multitudes of planets and life as you inhale and exhale. The sixth breath you take is for all life in the known universe. Finally, the seventh breath is for all dimensions, including time (past, present, future), all multi-verses, and all potential existence.

Big thought? Of course. But imagine what might take place inside of you if you were to begin every day thinking on a scale that size. Imagine how your everyday problems might shrink in the context of a meditation that grounds you in inhaling the pain and suffering of all living beings, past, present, and future, and then breathing back out a healing balm of energy to them. Imagine how you might transcend the immediate pain you have as you focus on the reality of the struggles faced by beings you don't even know about, let alone encounter. Seven Breaths has helped me develop an all-encompassing compassion that has transformed who I am and how I relate to the world by widening my perspective infinitely and by putting that vastness in my foreground on a daily basis.

Seven Breaths is a practical method for increasing the compassion you feel and exude. Imagine going through your day with the perspective that what you experience is only a minute fraction of the essence of the totality of existence. Seven Breaths is a deep exercise that can be done in a relatively short amount of time. At a minimum, it can improve the way you view, approach, and interact with others. At its best, Seven Breaths can reshape your ability to hold a macroperspective of life in the foreground of everything you experience. Although this meditation isn't a quick fix or a magic pill intended to produce euphoric feelings, in a fast-paced world where time management is valued, setting aside a few moments in your day to take seven intentional breaths is a worthwhile practice that can significantly impact the way you interact with others.

Compassion isn't weakness, and it certainly doesn't equate with giving in or being walked all over. Instead, it's a state of being that alters the energy you bring to interactions. Through compassion, your energy introduces your presence as a safe space for others. In the context of a safe space, people don't need to rely on defenses that might otherwise be on alert if they felt threatened or attacked. When you lead with compassion, you give yourself a significantly better chance to bypass defensiveness and communicate in ways that are heard.

Practicing Loving-Kindness

▶ A teacher once asked a group of students the following question: "If I gave you a bucket, what would you put in it?" The students asked what the bucket was for, but the teacher refused to give a context. He simply said, "I would just give you a bucket, and what I want to know is what you would put in it." A young man spoke up and answered, "I would put my cell phone in it." The teacher said, "Okay, great," and then pointed to another student. She said, "Food." Another student said, "Money." The teacher said, "Wonderful. So whatever you put in your bucket, you put in your bucket. I have no judgment about that. The point I want to make is this: Whatever you put in your bucket will in fact be in your bucket, right?" The students seemed confused, but they all agreed that, yes, whatever they put in their bucket would be in their bucket.

The teacher continued, "It might not seem profound to realize that whatever you put in your bucket will be in it, until you realize this: Your mind is the same way. Whatever you fill your mind with will be in your mind. If you watch violent movies and play violent games and listen to violent music, then expect violence to be in your mind. But if you fill your mind with peaceful images, peaceful music, and peaceful thoughts, then that will be in your mind. You would do well to understand that whatever you put in your mind will be in it." ◀

You master whatever you practice. If you practice reacting impulsively out of anger, you will get very good at that. Conversely, if you practice patience, you will master that. One of the best ways to become more compassionate is to practice loving-kindness, beginning with your thoughts. "Mind is the forerunner of all actions," taught the Buddha. When you learn to control your self-talk, you will master your emotions, including anger.

Anger causes suffering because it expects, demands, and desires. Like someone practicing acts of cyber-cowardice by spewing hateful or degrading comments on the Internet from a hidden place of anonymity, anger also seems to operate in the dark recesses of impulse. When we shine light on the thoughts that are occurring around anger, however, it changes. What is brought to the light cannot remain in the dark. When every view we have of the world includes compassionate loving-kindness, we begin to overcome the cowardly anger that we previously permitted to control us.

Practicing loving-kindness and exuding compassion in the face of anger, aggression, and even violence might seem like a misplaced juxtaposition, but in the context of a larger, inclusive perspective, it's possible to see them as two sides of the same coin. One of my favorite anecdotes from the great mythologist Joseph Campbell is actually not one of the myths he told but, rather, a story from his own life. He once had the good fortune to meet a great saint in India. When you meet such a person, tradition dictates that the guru does not offer answers unsolicited but only responds to questions (an ideal way to practice Yield Theory, by the way, as teaching with such a pedagogy puts you in a position to meet students exactly where they are intellectually). Joseph Campbell's question to the teacher was this: "If, as we know, all things are Brahman, are this divine energy, then why do we renounce the world, why do we renounce vice, why do we renounce stupidity? Why do we not see the divine shining through the most brutal, the most horrendous, the most stupid, and most dark?" The teacher responded, "For you and me, that is where it is." From the rest of his writings and teachings, it seems clear Joseph Campbell got that lesson. The two of them understood that compassion is a state of being driven by perspective.

One of the easiest, most straightforward ways to practice loving-kindness is to mentally repeat the phrase "loving-kindness" as frequently as possible. By practicing saying it in your mind, it becomes a habit, and you will find you can rely on it when you need it most. For example, if your mind races with angry, vengeful, or even hate-inspired thoughts, you can redirect the negative thoughts by allowing the phrase "loving-kindness" to become the mantra.

Filling your mind with this phrase allows any negative thoughts or statements to drift into the background and eventually to disappear. Being mindful of the Buddha's wisdom that you are becoming what you think, as well as recognizing that whatever you fill your mind with will be in your mind, gives you the opportunity to actively choose to engage in the type of self-talk that will most directly lead you to the psychological space where you want to be.

You don't have to use the word "loving-kindness," of course. You can use any words that direct your mind to where you want to be. But I personally have experienced a radical transformation in my own life since I started utilizing this phrase on a daily basis. I began repeating "loving-kindness" to myself when I found that not only were some of the stories of the people I worked with sticking with me after I left them, but also the anger and violence were beginning to have primacy in my mind. At first, I had to force myself to remember to say it. Once it became a habit, however, I found that I would be repeating it even when I wasn't using it to redirect my mind away from angry or unwanted thoughts.

Then I started to use it anytime I wanted to lead with compassion in my life, including regarding thoughts about myself. Like many people I've encountered, it can be much easier for me to be forgiving of others than I am of myself. That changed when I started practicing mentally saying the phrase, "loving-kindness." Soon, I realized that the more I repeated it to myself, the more it guided my every interaction. This practice has helped me maintain my center regardless of what is happening around me, and that in turn has shaped how I approach others.

Applying Compassion

Imagine encountering a person who disagrees with something that you believe strongly. The moment that disagreement occurs, your defense system goes on high alert, triggering electrical charges and chemical processes in your brain that signal you should protect yourself. With excess adrenaline and cortisol flowing through you in that moment, you could easily erupt in anger and go off on the person, stating all the facts that support what you believe. From your cartoon-world perspective, you could prove why the other person "shouldn't" think those thoughts. Then a series of real-world questions about changing others hits you like a rush of insight: "What will my being right do? Will my angrily proving others wrong change anything? Will they just drop their beliefs and convert to my way of thinking? Or will me proving I'm right just elicit defensiveness? And so what if I'm right? What does that mean for me? Will I get a gold star? Will my ego be fed and allow me to convince myself that I'm better than others? Do I even like people who think they're better than others?" And the flurry of questions brings a new level of awareness for you. You realize that, although your ego wants to be right, your essence would rather apply compassion and seek to understand.

Applying compassion is a way of life, and opportunities to practice it are everywhere. Think of news stories you see that involve celebrities or media personalities whom you don't like, people you don't even personally know. What makes you not like someone—especially someone you don't even know? Evaluating your judgments and why you might feel strongly about disliking others takes effort. Applying compassion takes effort, and it doesn't just happen in your interactions—it begins in your thoughts. Do you enjoy seeing others fail? Do you get a little boost in your step when you see a successful person's mishaps? It takes courage to confront your ego and challenge why you feel the need to hold on to your judgments.

I've sat with people who have committed unspeakably horrendous acts of violence. I've felt my stomach turn from reading case files, seeing pictures of victims, and listening to serial sadists proudly describe the pain they've inflicted. I would be remiss if I gave the illusion that it was easy for me to work with those who've done such reprehensible acts. But time and again, for twenty years, I've asked myself: What's the alternative? I could shame them to make my ego feel better, but I would do nothing to spark real change; in fact, I would likely give them more fuel to warrant hurting others in the future. Throughout my whole career, time and again, I've come to the conclusion that meeting anger with more anger doesn't actually change anything. By leading with compassion, I can meet others wherever they are, connect with their essence, and ignite change from there.

Of course, there are times to defend yourself if you're in physical danger, and leading with compassion never entails condoning violence, anger, or harm in any way. Being compassionate toward others does not mean eschewing consequences or not following through with setting firm boundaries. But if only your ego is in danger, then the most important question to ask yourself is: Do you want to actually influence others to change? If your answer is yes, then it's wise to recognize the transformative power of applying compassion. Remember that just as granite's overlapping minerals give it strength, the overlap among the components in Yield Theory give this approach strength. The "mineral" compassion is comprised of love. Being compassionate entails you seeking to understand, not taking others' pain personally, and recognizing that people are more than their actions. It also entails the desire to be helpful, supportive, and empowering. In that, the attitude of compassion is disarming.

When you operate from the perspective that the reason people hurt one another is that they are trapped in the darkness of the labyrinth, it becomes easier to see others with compassion. Regardless of whatever has happened, the past is over. It's unchangeable. But the future is as of yet unwritten. Adding anger or violence to the present only adds to the content of anger and violence in the universe for the future. Just as whatever you put in your mind is in your mind, whatever you say and do is your contribution to the bucket of content that comprises the universe. The world has enough anger in its bucket, and it could benefit greatly from your compassion.

Summary

The Buddha taught us the powerful truth that love and compassion are the keys to overcoming anger and hatred. That truth applies directly to the way you handle anger. With a nonjudgmental perspective of understanding and compassion, you will be able to effectively circumvent others' defenses and speak to them in ways that can be heard, even in the midst of the most intense anger episodes. Walking past proverbial gargoyles and straight through anger can be scary, but when you lead with the type of oceanic waves of compassion that the Buddha exuded to overcome the anger of the stomping elephant, you can feel confident that your energy will precede you in a way • that helps you lessen anger and ultimately transform it. Leading with compassion is more than a mere academic or intellectual exercise: It's a reliable path through which you can face any anger at any time.

> The Master helps people lose everything they know, everything they desire, and creates confusion in those who think that they know.
>
> **LAO TZU**

Nonattachment

Letting Go of Ego

One of the easiest, most straightforward ideas to understand about anger is this: The more you cling to your ideas while others oppose them, the angrier you'll be. The more you tie yourself emotionally to others, the more they, not you, set the course for how you feel and, ultimately, for what you do. When you approach the world as a constant learner, however, you remain open to new knowledge in every moment. When you view yourself as an individual entity connected with everyone but not tied to anyone, you can simultaneously increase your compassion and accept complete responsibility for your thoughts, speech, and actions. To be nonattached doesn't mean that you cannot have beliefs and opinions or be extraordinarily close with others; instead, it is a state of openness and a lack of rigidity. In this chapter, you will see how nonattachment holds the key to separating yourself from your ego and clears the way for you to see the world from others' perspectives without taking on their emotions. From a position of nonattachment, you can listen, validate, and explore options in the most effective way possible.

Although there is overlap among the seven fundamental components and each is as significant as the next in creating the full approach of Yield Theory, I would argue that practicing nonattachment probably separates those who utilize Yield Theory with the most fidelity from those who do not. There is a reason for that: Rigidly clinging to the parochial ego inherently limits your perspective and sets you up to remain trapped in your cartoon world, whereas nonattachment keeps you in constant, ongoing assessment of the real world. Attachment is like being tethered so closely to one side of the box that your nose is touching it, but believing you can see all the other sides anyway. Nonattachment, on the other hand, is like being unfettered and free to travel around the entire box.

Inflexibility and rigidity are characteristics of the ego, which most frequently feels threatened in conflict and breaks far more easily than a person's essence. The more rigid your ego is, the more defensive you become, because you fear constant attack. Nonattachment is a quality of confidence, because the less attached you are, the less desire you have to condemn or convert. A recent experience I had encapsulates the application of nonattachment.

▶ Speaking to a collegiate athletic team, I asked the group how many planets there are in our solar system. A young man responded, "Eight." I said, "Are you sure?" And he said with certainty, "I am sure." I asked, "How certain are you?" He said, "I would bet my life on it." I then asked him if he considered dwarf planets to be planets. He said, "What are dwarf planets?" I said, "Are you aware that there are dwarf planets in our solar system?" He said, "No." I said, "I recently read that the International Astronomical Union currently recognizes that there are at least five dwarf planets in our solar system and hundreds more on the outer rim." He said, "I didn't know that." I said, "A minute ago, you were so certain that there are only eight planets in our solar system that you were willing to bet your life on it, and now it looks like you're not as sure." He said, "I think I just learned that I shouldn't bet my life on things that I can't be certain about." I said, "What can you be certain about?" He replied, "That I should never bet my life on things ever again." And I said with a smile, "It seems like you're pretty certain about that . . ." He laughed. The group laughed. We all laughed. When people are awake, the absurdity of certainty is comical. ◀

Nonattachment is often misunderstood, as on the surface people sometimes take it to mean that they cannot have preferences or beliefs or that they must subscribe to the idea that nothing is certain (which of course is in and of itself a certainty). To the contrary, nonattachment is about recognizing that every moment provides an opportunity for you to encounter information that might give you a more comprehensive perspective. If you view nonattachment from the context of the box metaphor I presented earlier, then it is about being open to realizing that in any given instance you might see a side or angle of the box that you previously didn't see.

To recognize that you have only partial knowledge can be scary if your ego—your cartoon-world perspective—is telling you that you "should" have more or complete knowledge. If, on the other hand, you view the world as a journey in which you are collecting knowledge along the way until the very end, then you can be open to picking up new information or even new angles on previous knowledge in every moment. That openness comes when you have the discipline and strength to set your ego aside and listen and learn with humble curiosity. When you understand that everyone you meet can teach you something that will contribute to your having the broadest possible perspective, then being the eternal student becomes exciting. To that end, the attitude you can carry into every encounter is: "Teach me. Teach me about your perspective. Teach me what you see. Teach me, because I genuinely want to learn."

Most reasonable people are quick to admit that they still have more to learn in life; interestingly enough, however, the moment you disagree with them, their defenses rise. If people genuinely believed that they still have more to learn, then there would be no need for them to be defensive when others presented alternative ideas. Perhaps more importantly to your own life: If *you* genuinely believe that you still have more to learn, then it's wise to hold that thought in your foreground. The less attached you are to already knowing, the more open you'll remain to listening and learning rather than defending. Also, the less attached you are in the way you present information to others, the fewer barriers you place between the ideas you have and the person with whom you're communicating. It's often your ego's desire to be certain that places an immediate need to be right ahead of the overarching goal of learning.

The Buddha taught millennia ago that suffering stems from desire. The more we desire something and believe we "should" have it, the more we suffer if we don't have it. If we're in physical pain and desire to be pain free, for example, we suffer. If we want others to live according to our cartoon worlds and they don't, we suffer. In this way, it's suffering that leads to anger and conflict. Desire and attachment go hand in hand. The more we desire others to believe what we believe, think the way we think, and do the things we want them to do, the more upset we become (that is, the more we suffer) when they don't think, believe, or behave in the manner we want.

Desire in and of itself, of course, is not wrong or bad, and not all desire causes suffering. After all, the desire to learn about others can help us connect with them. The desire for enlightenment can lead us to a path of peace. So just because desire can cause suffering doesn't mean it always does. Being attached to needing to be nonattached, then, is another form of attachment.

Balance is the key, and so is awareness. It's wise to be aware that the more attached you are to anything (from people to things to ideas), the more upset you'll likely be if something gets between you and your attachment.

There are two areas where your attachment to desire can impede your communication and increase anger and conflict. The first is the degree to which you are attached to what you believe; the second is the degree to which you have convinced yourself that you need others to see things your way or do what you demand (that is, live according to your cartoon world). Others can pick up on how attached you are to what you believe just as easily as you can pick up on it in them. Tense body language and facial movements give away rigidity in thinking, and so does talking over others and/or not incorporating what others are sharing in your replies. The more others see that you have an agenda in regard to what you want from them, the more likely they are to be defensive.

Being nonattached to your ideas is one of the most effective ways to circumvent others' fight-or-flight response, but it takes a level of maturity and esteem to handle others disagreeing with the ideas you present. The less attached you are to what you say, though, the more permission others feel to objectively evaluate what you're saying without the pressure of needing to agree with you.

Imagine that all of the ideas, thoughts, and beliefs that you have ever had in your entire life were able to be magically fitted into one handheld book. Now imagine that you are holding that book tightly against your body. When someone disagrees with anything in the book that you're clinging tightly to (as though it is a part of you), you will feel personally attacked, as if they're disagreeing with a part of who you are. But if you really do embrace the belief that you always have more to learn, then you can see that *you are not your ideas*, because every moment has the potential to bring you new information that can add to or otherwise alter what you think, know, and believe. You are indeed separate from your book, and clinging to it is optional. Imagine then that instead of clinging tightly to your book, you can set it down, away from you. Now, when others disagree with anything or everything that's in your book, you can plainly see that it's *not* a personal attack against your being. The less attached you are to your book, the less defensive you'll be when others view things differently. This is nonattachment.

Nonattachment in Listening

Professional kickboxers have a big enough challenge fighting in the ring, but imagine if they had to fight their opponent while remaining attached by a very short rope to their corner. The more tightly they're attached to their corner, the less slack they would have, and the less they would be able to move around and use their full skill set. Similarly, the more attached you are to your ideas, the more difficult it is to be open, rational, and able to tap into your full intellectual skill set. Clinging too tightly to your ego prevents you from learning. This is especially true in regard to listening. Listening in a nonattached way in the most pragmatic sense means being able to set aside your confirmation biases, assumptions, and even what you might be primed to hear. It's important to hear what others are *actually* communicating versus what you believe they're communicating, but if you are attached to what you believe they'll say or if you hold fast to your ego and define yourself by what you already think you know, it will be scary to listen in a nonattached way.

Whereas you might smile lightheartedly at watching a toddler cover his ears in an attempt to refuse to hear that it's time to clean up his toys, the unfortunate reality is that adults have their own way of throwing psychological tantrums when their egos are challenged. In a famous example of attachment to ideas and the status quo, Professor Giulio Libri, a contemporary of Galileo, refused to look through the telescope for fear that what he might see would nullify what he believed about the sun. "How ridiculous!" you might think—until you look at how you've responded to those who have challenged things like your own political and religious viewpoints through the years. Being attached to what you already believe stops you from seeing and hearing what you have the potential to learn.

One of the biggest challenges we face in conflict is how attached people are to their side of the box. Attachment limits what you're able to see. We know that many arguments ensue and persist because people are talking about apples and oranges. Perhaps more startling is the fact that, even when people are talking only about apples, things escalate when they don't realize that they and the person they're arguing with are viewing those apples through opposite ends of the same pair of binoculars. To one the apples seem small, to another, large—and each is correct. I can say the sky is blue, and you can agree with me, but we cannot fully know each other's experience of the word "blue." The color blue has many shades, and my eyes might be transmitting a slightly different shade to me than yours are to you.

This concept of similar but different was at the center of an Internet meme controversy around a photograph of a striped dress in 2015. Some people saw "the dress" as white-gold; others saw it as blue-black. People were attached to what they saw, and even argued their side, because they did not understand that our eyes send signals to our brains that experience colors differently. The ultimate truth about the dress is that it's no color at all; technically, it only reflects a wavelength of light that our eyes send as information to our brain to interpret how it appears to us. It's a simple demonstration that we see with our brains and not our eyes. Yes, the solution to what was a relatively fun conflict is that simple; but consider the innumerable not-so-fun conflicts that you've experienced in your life. Imagine if you could have approached all of them from the understanding that people have different perceptions, in part because our senses process information differently, but also because our cognitive functioning, our ability to process emotions, and our life experiences all lead us to experiencing the world differently as well. Acknowledging the many complexities of every conflict is the cornerstone of Yield Theory, because it emphasizes the multiple perspectives that exist.

Through the years, I've heard many people exclaim, "I don't want to acknowledge the complexities! Sometimes things are just wrong, and I don't care!" I call that frustration. It makes tremendous sense that we would rather simplify things and make life easier for ourselves. We don't want to think that a sex offender was himself perpetrated on many times before he acted out on others; we would rather call him "sick," put him out of our minds, and move on with our lives. Or, for a perhaps more relatable example, picture a family member whom you simply don't agree with. "What side could they possibly have that I don't already know?" you ask. That's the point. Your family member, your loved one, and even that person thrown out of your mind—*they all have a side.* They have more to their story than you see, just as you have more to your story than what others see.

To set your ego and perspective aside in order to genuinely listen in a nonattached way can be challenging. Keeping in mind the metaphor of the box is a practical way for you to let go of the assumption that you know what others are about to say and instead listen to what they are actually communicating. There are ways to show your nonattachment through active listening, such as verbally acknowledging what people are saying, as well as giving nonverbal cues, such as nodding your head, making eye contact, and using body language. An important sign of nonattachment through active listening is not speaking over others. Even more telling to people you're interacting with, incorporating what they say into your response shows them that you were genuinely listening to what they were expressing. Checking your listening is always part of the second core action of validation.

Nonattachment in Validation

There's another effective way to demonstrate nonattachment when you validate or even reflect what you're hearing: verbally acknowledging your willingness to let go of what you thought someone said if they correct you or otherwise demonstrate that what you heard was inaccurate. "You know what? You're right. I was off with the way I saw that, so thanks for sticking with me and saying it again. I think I see what you're saying now." When people correct you about what they said or how they feel, they usually do so because either you misheard them or else you accurately heard them but they feel exposed or vulnerable about what they just said. When I see people backtrack, I immediately assess whether I might have heard them accurately or not. If I sense I have heard them accurately and they might be backtracking, I try to give them an out. Again, think push-pull from aikido: As they pull away, I push. Me giving others an out regarding what they said is not the same as me permitting them to get away with an unacceptable behavior. Instead, when it's only a matter of people backtracking on what they're sharing, I help them have that out, and then I assess where they are in their level of understanding, stage of change, or preparedness to disclose information or assume responsibility. By letting go of needing others to admit they were wrong about what they said, you will find it much easier to make an accurate assessment.

So to implement nonattachment in validation: Reflect back what you hear others say, be open to their redirection, be mindful to assess where they are, and then of course be open to being wrong about your entire perception.

Nonattachment in Exploring Options

Nonattachment is a critical tool in helping others think through their viable choices. Especially in times of conflict, the more attached you are to pushing others to do what you want them to do, the more resistant they seem to become. Conversely, the less attached you are to what you present, the safer you make others feel about choosing whichever option most resonates with them. The goal is to guide people, not to direct them; it's to steer them down a road while keeping *them* in the driver's seat. Specifically, in Yield Theory, the idea is to explore options with others and then let go. It's to internally motivate people to make the types of choices that most effectively help *them* handle conflict.

Individuals alone are accountable for their choices. The only part we play in communication is to present potential options; the choice to act always lies with the individual. As much as I hope that others make the peaceful choice, I recognize that this desire is simply reflective of my cartoon world, and I cannot make others choose anything. I can, however, be responsible for implementing the consequences that follow others' choices. The more attached you are to what you offer others, the more personally you'll take it if or when they choose differently. Being attached to the options you provide is extremely counterproductive, because your attachment creates unnecessary conflict for people to encounter. In other words, if people have to overcome whatever conflict they face *and* your ego, then you have only added to their conflict, not lessened it.

It can be helpful to visualize the options you propose for others to consider as pages in your "book" of ideas. If you cling too tightly to your ideas, as though they are a part of you, then any disagreement with your ideas will likely trigger your biological drive to defend yourself. But if you can set your "book" of ideas—the options you propose—off to the proverbial side, offering them without attaching yourself to whatever others decide, then it will be easier for you to realize that people's resistance to your ideas is not equivalent to them attacking you. The less attached you are to your ideas, the more you will realize that people disagreeing with you or not accepting your ideas does not put you in physical danger, so there is no reason for you to be defensive or offended if they don't like, accept, or use your proposed options. In so doing, you can observe their actions with interest, and you can learn a lot about where they really are in their readiness or willingness to change. When you can move your intellectual understanding that people disagreeing with the options you highlight for them doesn't mean that they are disagreeing with who you are as a person into your physical practice, then you will free yourself from being reactive when others disagree with you or don't follow your advice.

Let's say that you favor a particular political candidate whom your good friend does not support. When you explain why you favor this candidate, your friend still says she does not agree. The more attached you are to needing her to agree with you, the more upset you'll be when she sees things differently. The more you convince yourself that she "has to" believe what you do, the bigger the divide you put between you and her. To physically practice nonattachment is to present your ideas and let them go. It's to share what you see with your friend but entirely respect that she might be seeing a different side of the box than you see. And the same is true with any beliefs you share or advice you give.

Huffing and puffing or otherwise complaining that people don't follow your advice comes from attachment to ego. When you take others not following your advice personally, you make *their* life choices about *your* ego; but just as your decisions in life have not been about anyone other than you, the same is true for others. Our egos are influenced by a sense of omnipotence that tries to convince us we're somehow responsible for what other people do. We're not. What others do is not a reflection of you; it's a reflection of them.

When you listen and validate with compassion and in authentically nonattached ways, people lower their defenses and move away from the emotional center of their brains. As others begin to open themselves up to alternative options beyond their initial impulsive reactions, you can help dismantle the certainty their anger has created and open them up to alternate options. Relying on nonattached language to challenge people is the key. In other words, you can help them move away from their anger-driven certainty, or "create confusion," as Lao Tzu says, by using phrases such as "I wonder if it would help to . . ." or "It seems like one option you might have is . . ." By using words like "wonder" and "seems like," you don't provide much to rail against. Instead, from a place of authenticity, you are literally "just wondering" if the thought that came to your mind might be helpful. The less attached you are to the option you are raising, the less defensive they have to be in responding.

Since Yield Theory is about getting around the anger and defensiveness of others so that you can speak in a way that is actually heard, using nonattached language is a skill that's important to develop. Here are some additional nonattached phrases that can help you remove unnecessary barriers between you and others in the midst of conflict:

- "I thought I heard you say . . ."

- "My memory of it was . . ."

- "From my perspective, it seemed like . . ."

- "I think I remember you saying
  something to the effect of . . ."

- "I'm not sure of the exact words you used, but my
  memory was it was something along the lines of . . ."

- "It's definitely possible I could be off, but
  what I remember was . . ."

By fully owning your experience alone, you can avoid being trapped in arguments about who's "right" or "wrong" and stay focused on moving through the conflict and ultimately learning from it.

In Zen Buddhism, nonattachment is referred to as "the soap of the teachings." Soap serves a purpose when you wash clothes, but eventually you need to rinse that soap out and move on to the larger goal, which is to have clean clothes. In the same way, the goal of communication is to get to the heart of the process and learn what you can from it. Remaining attached to the specifics is like leaving the soap in the clothes.

Although soap is a large contributor to what makes clothes clean, the reality is that they are not entirely clean until the soap is gone. I see our thoughts the same way. Our thoughts can serve us well, but they can take us only as far as the penultimate destination—the ultimate destination is experience. Your language, at best, will help you connect with others; eventually, however, you'll move beyond language to sheer experience.

Nonattachment as Emotional Freedom

To be truly nonattached is to genuinely respect people's autonomy. That is very difficult for many people, because it seems natural for us to want others to abide by our cartoon-world rules. One of the most helpful concepts I use to teach what nonattachment in communication looks like comes from the work of pioneering psychiatrist Murray Bowen. He described *differentiation* as the process by which individuals become uniquely themselves. Differentiation is the antithesis of *enmeshment*. To be enmeshed with others is to be emotionally tied to them. For example, if you are enmeshed with someone and that person gets really sad, mad, or anxious, then you will also soon be sad, mad, or anxious. The challenge enmeshment poses for us is that we have a tendency to lose ourselves by being swept up in others' experiences. We do not realize that we can show compassion and interest without being tied to what others are feeling.

Enmeshment and differentiation can be understood through a simple Aesop's fable.

▶ A frog and a mouse were such great friends that they decided they should tie themselves together so that they could never be far apart. So that's just what they did: They got a string and tied their legs together.

Now, things were fine for a time while they were out of the water, and it certainly seemed like a good idea at first, because these two companions got to be together always. Eventually, however, the frog missed the water, as was his nature. When he dived back in, the mouse, still tied to him, drowned.

The drowned body of the mouse floated back up to the surface of the water. A hawk saw it, swooped down for the easy meal, and also ate the frog as well. ◀

The moral of this story is to be mindful whom you tie yourself to, because it might not be in your best interest to always go where they go. But beyond that moral, this tale provides insight about what it means to be enmeshed versus differentiated. The string that tied the frog and the mouse together represents enmeshment. If one went here, so did the other; and in Aesop's tale, being tied together ultimately led to their demise. It would have been completely possible, however, for the mouse and the frog to remain close yet not be tied to each other. Had they remained unfettered, when the frog returned to the water, the mouse could have done something different. Being apart did not mean they would have cared less about each other, and of course both would have survived longer. To be connected and close but not emotionally tied to others' ups and downs is differentiation.

Enmeshment and differentiation occur on a continuum and have nothing to do with being good or bad or right or wrong. When we are born, we very much rely on caretakers to help us survive, so we naturally begin our lives enmeshed. In fact, a mother being in tune with her baby's various cries helps her take care of her child's different needs. Of course, eventually children grow up, have the option to move away, and may begin families of their own. Distance, however, does not equate to differentiation, and neither does disengagement or disagreement. For example, if people move far away from family simply *to be away*, then they are still emotionally enmeshed, even if they remain disengaged or don't communicate. The "I'm too reactive around you so I need to get away" mentality expresses enmeshment. Similarly, if people feel the need to prove they're different by doing the opposite of what the family members they dislike would do, that, too, is enmeshment.

In the most extreme sense of enmeshment, to be enmeshed is to no longer have feelings that are yours alone. For example, an inmate once told me that he "never had a feeling of his own until he was in prison." He was so enmeshed with his mother that if she became angry, he became angry; if she was enraged with others, he would automatically become enraged with them as well. Although we all experience enmeshment to some degree, there are certainly varying degrees of it. It's natural to be tied to others' emotions in some way, and in the very, very rare cases where someone has no connection whatsoever to others' emotions, we define that as sociopathic.

To be differentiated is to be emotionally connected but not tied to others. It is a cognitive and emotional recognition of the self as separate. In other words, I can love someone in my family a great deal, and if that person becomes very sad, I don't have to become sad with that person; instead, I can be there as a source of peace for them. I never have to actually have other people's experiences in order to lead with compassion and listen, validate, and explore options with them. To be nonattached is not to not care; rather, it means you are not tied to living out the emotions of others.

In a very real sense, to be differentiated or nonattached means having the ability to become a place of peace for those around you. For example, I care very much about others in my life and about what happens to them, but I fully recognize the limitations of what control I realistically have. By avoiding getting swept up in believing that I have more control than I actually do, I am able to give people genuine kindness, compassion, and nonjudgmentalness, as I respect the free will that they have to choose anything they want. And by not tying myself to others emotionally, I am able to maintain the kind of energy that can be most beneficial to them.

To be nonattached, then, is to be free from seeing others as an extension of your emotional self, which allows you to give compassion without conditions or demands or expectations. For example, I once told a woman who was in a verbally abusive relationship, "You can choose to stay in this relationship if you want, and you certainly will not get any judgment from me, but I guess my hope is that you will at least allow yourself to consider the possibility that you don't have to." I continued, "And if you're not in the space yet to consider that, then that's completely okay, too." I told her that I recognized she was already under pressure to think and act in certain ways by the person who was abusing her, so the last thing I wanted to do was force any unnecessary pressure on her, even if that pressure was for her to be free.

By acknowledging that the choice she was already making was completely acceptable, I was able to effectively circumvent her fight-or-flight response, get around any sense of shame she felt for not having left her partner, and help her feel safe enough to actually explore the possibility of making a different choice. She was already suffering though verbal abuse; I did not want to add to her suffering by telling her she "had" to do something she might not be ready to do. Although I personally did not want this consenting adult to choose to stay in an abusive relationship, I maintain the highest respect for people's right to make their own decisions. It's not my role to dictate to others how they "should" live their lives; instead, through the lens of Yield Theory, I view it as my job to merge with others in order to compassionately see the world from their perspective and then help them explore the best possible options for themselves.

The ability to remain differentiated and nonattached, even when you strongly hope that others make a particular decision that they're currently not making, requires that you be mindful of your own cartoon world, as well as that you respect the free will of others without imposing your demands on them. Of course, no matter the decisions that any of us make, consequences are always inevitable. Using this approach with the woman who was in the abusive relationship, by the way, opened up a path for her that eventually led to her choosing to leave that relationship, as well as learning how to set firm boundaries in subsequent relationships. (She has now been happily married in a very healthy relationship for ten years.) All my interactions with her centered on listening, validating with compassion, and then ultimately exploring options without attachment.

Applying Nonattachment

Nonattachment involves letting go of your ego's grip on its certainty of the situation. In other words, whereas your ego will speak convincingly to you that your perception is the "correct" one, when you practice nonattachment you're able to question that certainty. Think about the way you take feedback. If someone tells you that you came across differently in an interaction from how you had perceived yourself, then applying nonattachment involves you letting go of your own perception enough to genuinely consider the feedback that's being given to you.

Picture someone saying that you were rude in a situation where you honestly did not mean to be, try to be, or even experience yourself as coming across as rude. Here are two different ways you could respond to that feedback.

From your ego: "No, I wasn't!" or "You're wrong."

Applying nonattachment: "I honestly didn't feel myself being rude, but I'm open to the idea that if that's how I was perceived, that person must have picked up on something I wasn't aware of."

The ego wants to control situations, but more than that, the ego seeks to control perception. Controlling perception, however, occurs only in the cartoon world. In the real world, we cannot control other people's perceptions. Applying nonattachment helps us live out the reality that we cannot control others' perceptions, and it gives us an opportunity to consistently seek to learn how to be as effective as possible in the world that actually exists.

When you really focus on controlling only what you can, it becomes easier to let go of trying to control the outcome. Being nonattached as you listen to and interact with others does not mean you have to acquiesce to whatever's said or even change your perception. You can, for instance, as in the example above, maintain your own perception of your experience that you didn't feel like you were being rude; but by being nonattached, you can genuinely respect that others' perceptions are different from your own, and you may even gain a grain of insight that might lead to you interacting more effectively in the future.

Although it can be relatively easy to understand the concept of nonattachment, the reality is that it can take tremendous effort to practice. Your ego, after all, has spent a lifetime creating a cartoon world, and it's convinced that the cartoon world really is the way the world should be. Practicing nonattachment, however, is psychologically freeing, because you no longer have to expend energy trying to force the real world into your cartoon world (and continuously letting yourself down). Nonattachment is also liberating energy for others to be around, because they don't have to rail against someone trying to force them to abide by an unrealistic cartoon world.

Nonattachment does not equal a laissez-faire attitude of "who cares whatever happens." Instead, it's letting go of your need for life to work out the way you believe it should. Interestingly, when you let go of being attached to your cartoon world and approach others without a need for them to think or act in any one particular way, their defenses drop. With their guard down, they don't need to defend their position and can move more rapidly from emotional defensiveness to higher-level thinking and decision-making.

Here's an annotated example of me applying Yield Theory in an interaction with an angry man. I explain in parentheses why I said the things I did.

During a brief intermission in a two-hour anger management group, an irate man I'll call "John" approached me. He was furious because his parole officer tested his urine for drug use three days in a row. Although it's well within the rights of parole officers to test their parolees as often as they suspect drug use, it's not typical for such tests to be administered for three consecutive days. John believed that the only reasons he was being tested frequently was because "the system is corrupt" and because he believed his ex-girlfriend had called to request it. His face was red, he was visibly agitated, and his tone of voice was loud.

> **Me:** "What's up?" (Never say seven words when three will suffice. Saying, "What's up?" allows me to say less and listen more.)

> **John:** "I'm so furious! Don't even try to calm me down, because what happened to me was so messed up!"

> **Me:** "I have no desire to calm you down. What happened?" (Expressing that I have no desire to calm him down reflects me using nonattachment. I really was not trying to calm him down. Instead, my intention was to interact with him in the most effective way possible and help him calm himself down. The difference is subtle but profound.)

> **John:** "The whole system is so corrupt! My ex gets everything she wants, and she's messing with me—and she has the police on her side!"

> **Me:** "That sounds messed up." (Saying that something "sounds" messed up is not agreeing that something *is* messed up, but rather acknowledging that if I was seeing it as he was, it certainly "sounded" that way.)

John: "Don't even try to calm me down, because I have every right to be this angry! They're corrupt!"

Me: "Man, I'm not going to try to calm you down, because I actually know that feeling of having people gang up on me. What happened exactly, though?" (I shared with him that I know the feeling of having people gang up on me because I do know that feeling, albeit in a different way.)

John: "They tested me three days in a row."

Me: "Man, three days in a row?" (My tone of voice in the way I reflected his statement was in and of itself a validation.)

John: "Yes." (I shook my head back and forth as he spoke.) He reiterated with force, "I refuse to calm down, because I shouldn't have to take what they're doing!"

Me (recognizing that the break was almost over and we didn't have much time for this interaction): "I'm not going to try to calm you down in any way. I mean, three days in a row is a lot . . . I'm just wondering, if we were standing here in a week talking about this, what might you be saying to yourself about the situation?" (By going with his energy and not insisting that he needed to calm down, I was able to create confusion in his certainty, which is a lead-in for him to begin helping himself. I wanted to deliver it in a way that he was open to hearing.)

John: "I guess if it was a week from now, I'd probably say that I might have overreacted."

Me: "Maybe, but maybe not; I really don't know. But I guess I just wonder, if it was a month from now, what you'd be saying to yourself?" (By saying, "Maybe, but maybe not," I was not forcing that insight or making it about something he had to get in that moment. Again, going with his energy—think push-pull from aikido—I gave him nothing to resist, which allowed me to take his higher-level cognitive decision-making to the next level.)

John (his face visibly less red now): "Well, a month from now, I guess I would probably say that I was on parole, and I guess they had a right to test me every single day if they want."

Me: "Man, that's insightful. For you to come to that in the middle of being this angry . . . So let's just take it a step further and say that it's a year from now. I wonder what you'd say to yourself about all this then?" (I overtly praised the insight I wanted to reinforce, and then I also gave a subconscious message of reinforcement regarding his ability to think insightfully in the midst of his intense emotion, both of which prepared him to hear a final level of conscious insight.)

John (now calm, as evidenced by a slower cadence in his voice and with no redness in his face): "A year from now I would probably look back on this moment and say, 'Man, I still had a lot to learn back then.'"

Me (smiling): "We're going to start group back up now, but honestly, I think you're probably a lot further along than you think." (I expressed to him that he was further along than he might have thought to empower him to reflect on the way he was able to calm himself down, move through this experience, and learn by tapping into his authentic self, rather than remaining locked in his ego.) He walked away completely calm, and I even noticed him smiling and shaking his head shortly thereafter, almost as if he was replaying our interaction in his mind.

Living Nonattachment

Think about something that you believed deeply when you were very young, but as you got older and learned more about the world, you altered that belief. At the time you believed it strongly, and it would have been difficult for you to encounter those who challenged your thinking. Now think of your current beliefs. In this present moment of your life, you likely feel as strongly about your current beliefs as you did when you were young and tied to that belief you have long since shed. Of course it's possible that what you believe now is absolute truth and that you simultaneously see all sides of the box regarding every topic you hold dear; but the other possibility is that even your most cherished beliefs are not absolute truth.

Whereas an extremist might bounce from one extreme to the other—"Oh, well, if what I believe might not be true, then I guess nothing is true and we can never know anything!"—I would advocate for a more balanced, less reactive experience of nonattachment. It's not that you cannot know anything; it's that regardless of what you understand in any given moment, there always exist other perspectives that might not have occurred to you yet. This attitude of openness is in line with your authentic self being driven to constantly grow.

A rock climber en route up a mountainside might cling firmly to the rocks in front of her, and understandably so. But if she's not willing to reach for new places to grab, she will either remain stuck where she is or be forced to descend the mountain. Yes, the rocks she currently holds and her footing might be solid, but until she's completed her climb, there is still higher mountainside to scale. Likewise, as long as you are alive, there is still more for you to learn. Clinging to your current perspective will always inhibit growth. Nonattachment allows you to keep searching for new rocks that permit you to continually climb higher up the mountain of your life.

Bruce Lee, when describing his own approach to martial arts, once said, "Absorb what is useful, discard what is useless, and add what is specifically your own." His words encapsulate my perspective on offering Yield Theory to you. The seven fundamental components are pieces that are foundational for practicing Yield Theory with fidelity, but within the framework of the methodology I offer is the freedom for you to be uniquely yourself. The ever-present goal is circumventing others' defensiveness so you can communicate in ways that can be heard, and the seven fundamental components are keys to doing that. The way in which you cling to or discard what resonates with you or not, however, is entirely up to you.

If I ever got so wrapped up in Yield Theory that I declared Yield Theory to be "the" way, rather than "a" way, then I would be missing the point of nonattachment. Throughout this book there will be some pieces that resonate with you more than others, and there will be sections that apply more aptly to your life at different times. All that's perfectly natural.

Practicing nonattachment means being open to the possibility that you are off base every time you communicate. It's not saying that you will be inaccurate or that you cannot be accurate, only that you are genuinely open to seeing another side of the box, one that, as a human being with a limited vantage point, you simply could not otherwise see. That constant willingness to learn contributes to humility, and humble, kind energy is the key to compassion, which is, of course, the heart of Yield Theory.

As you begin to practice nonattachment with intentionality, be mindful to note how others respond to you. Yes, it will take effort to set your ego aside and let go of the ever-present cartoon-world perspective your ego creates, but the more you practice it, the more it will become second nature. Living out the fundamental component of nonattachment will help you circumvent others' defensiveness and navigate your way through conflict; it will also help you experience a great sense of emotional freedom.

Summary

You don't need to be attached to an outcome to be invested in the energy you put into giving others your best. The less attached you are to your perspective, the less defensive you'll need to be if and when others challenge it. By seeing yourself as a constant learner, you can avoid attachment to what you believe you know in the present moment. Nonattachment isn't about not believing anything, not caring, or not being invested in your thoughts or beliefs; instead, it's centered on letting go of your ego's grip and continuously being open to the potential personal growth each new experience of life brings.

The gentlest thing in the world overcomes
the hardest thing in the world.
LAO TZU

Conscious Education

Plato's Cave and the Expansion
of Understanding

Listening with openness and compassion as you validate others' experiences is the cornerstone of meeting people where they are, yielding to their energy, and connecting with them, but those two core actions are simply not enough to help you get all the way through anger. Exploring options is the critical third piece in handling anger, and it is in this core action that you can add to the insight and knowledge others have. On the other side of anger is understanding, and insight is the quickest way to move from emotion to reason in a blink.

Conscious education is how you get there. Conscious education means expanding awareness—both others' and your own. It involves learning and then sharing the kind of practical information that helps you and others steer away from instinctive reactions to anger and down a different path. It is about the essential truths underlying the way we respond to anger and how understanding these essential truths leads to the personal development necessary for more effectively handling anger and conflict.

Resistance and narrow-mindedness are the vital organs of anger. That is why skeptical people are quick to assert that nothing can really be done for angry people who don't want to change. "You can lead a horse to water," they say, "but you cannot make him drink." And that might be true; however, we can certainly put salt in his oats and make him pretty darn thirsty! Similarly, although you cannot make others have insight, you can present logical, useful information to them that entices them to want to learn more. Put another way, with conscious education directed at sparking insight in ways that resonate with people, you can capture others' attention and draw them in like a moth to a flame.

Whether you're putting salt in others' oats or lighting a flame that draws them in, both metaphors suggest the same key to conscious education: Present information in a way that taps into the internal drive of others and leads them in the healthiest and most peaceful direction possible. In short, presenting valuable and pragmatic information to people that is immediately applicable to their lives and meaningful for them is the salt that will motivate them to drink from the waters of resolution and peace.

As you have seen already in this book, authenticity in interactions matters. That is why there are two crucial aspects to conscious education. The first involves applying the information in this chapter to your own life so that you practice what you preach. It involves you learning what's presented in these pages, sitting with it, and then integrating this wisdom in ways that widen your perspective and help you navigate through anger and conflict. The second aspect to the fundamental component of conscious education is sharing this information with others at the right time and in the most effective way, especially when they are in the midst of their own difficult emotions.

Plato's Cave

It can be challenging to set your own perspective aside and try to see what others see. It becomes even more challenging when your beliefs are steeped in the feeling of certainty. So it makes a lot of sense that inviting others to see the world differently is rarely easy; it is even more difficult in times of anger and conflict. Despite our actual capacity for expanded consciousness, we tend to remain locked in restricted world views. The clearest image I ever found to explain why this is so comes from the legendary philosopher Plato's famous allegory of the cave. His allegory is an apt description for the ego.

In book 25 of his *Republic*, Plato poses a frightening hypothetical scenario of what might happen if prisoners were chained inside a cave from the time they were infants. In addition to this horrific confinement, he asks readers to imagine that the prisoners' heads are positioned in such a way that they cannot see behind them. These prisoners face the back interior of the cave wall, while a perpetual fire burns outside of the cave, casting shadows of passersby on the wall in front of the captives. The prisoners would grow up their entire lives hearing the voices of humans but only ever seeing shadows corresponding with those voices. In time, Plato says, the prisoners would come to know the shadows as reality.

The key to this allegory lies in what Plato asks next: What would happen if we took one of those prisoners as an adult and freed him? After making his way out of the cave and struggling to see in the light, imagine the amount of fear he might encounter when he saw the immensity of wide open spaces or, worse, when he saw three-dimensional human beings talking instead of the shadows that he knew all his life. No doubt he would be so shocked by the outside world, he would want to retreat to the cave and the shadow world that he knew all his life.

Before we judge this prisoner for what would seem to us like foolishness—to reimpose a prison sentence on himself—we would do well to understand that we also live in our own psychological caves. When we are presented with information that contradicts what we believe we know, we often retreat behind defense mechanisms that keep us safely locked in our egos. Our egos, then, can be thought of as our own personal psychological caves, and the shadows we see cast on the cave walls are the certainties that we have about the world.

Conscious education centers on expanding the way we see the world. The word "conscious" comes from the Latin *conscius*, meaning "knowing, aware," which in turn is derived from *com*, "with" or "thoroughly," and *scire*, "to know"; essentially, consciousness equates awareness. The word "education" comes from the Latin root *ducere*, which means "to lead," and *ex*, meaning "out." So the heart of conscious education is to lead out by increasing awareness. In the context of Plato's cave, we have a powerful visual for what conscious education looks like, as well as a reasonable understanding of why people are resistant to taking in new information—to leaving the cave.

From a biological evolutionary perspective, anger can lead to conflict, and conflict can lead to death; and although that might seem a bit extreme, from the vantage point of the brain's instinct to survive, it's really not that farfetched at all. When people are angry or in conflict, their vision narrows, and they tend to think impulsively and often irrationally. The goal of conscious education is to help them explore options that are alternatives to the impulsive ones their anger is driving them to consider.

In 2010, researchers Brendan Nyhan and Jason Reifler discovered and defined what they call the "backfire effect" to describe the phenomenon of people becoming more defensive of their beliefs when they're presented with information that counters those beliefs. In other words, instead of changing our perspectives in the face of evidence, our beliefs only grow stronger (that is, we retreat to the inside of the cave). Presenting new information to people, especially information that contradicts what they believe, is difficult enough, but throw in the emotion of anger, and the walls of defensiveness rise higher than ever. Offering conscious education to others in conflict takes considerable finesse. That's where listening and validating come into play, as well as creativity (which we will explore in the next chapter). Being able to circumvent others' fight-or-flight response and avoid the backfire effect are enormously important for delivering conscious education in a way that can be heard.

Let's say, for example, that I am faced with someone who has a problem with anger. If I come right out and tell her she has an anger problem, it will likely elicit defensiveness through rationalizations and justifications. Instead, I choose to merge with her, listen, validate, and then offer this insight: "I wonder what people are seeing in you that they would even suggest you struggle with anger. I mean, we could probably both agree that if multiple people are saying something to you, it's not likely coming out of nowhere, so let's honestly think together about what they could potentially be seeing." By leading with authentic compassion and phrasing my observation in this nonattached way, I'm offering her the salt that can lead her to search her memory for the ways others have given her feedback about her anger in the past. Even if she just feels motivated to search for an answer, she is essentially drinking the water. For someone who had previously denied or was otherwise unaware that she had a problem with anger, being presented with conscious information in a nonattached way makes it easier to consider.

Remember, your cartoon-world view will demand that others "should" have the information you have (or you believe they should have), whereas your real-world view will help you assess what others actually do know, meet them where they are, and then share the information you hope for them to have in ways that actually work for them.

Insight is one of the most valuable gifts we have and can share, but helping to spark insight in those who are angry takes work. The more you know and the better you truly understand what you know, the more ways you have to teach it. Conscious education as a whole extends infinitely beyond what is shared here, as it entails *any* information outside of people's psychological caves that can help them in their path of personal development. The following section, however, encapsulates the teachings that I see as most central to Yield Theory.

Essential Wisdom

I call this section "Essential Wisdom" because these are the core concepts and insights that can transform anger. When you understand the information presented in this section well enough that you can teach it to everyone—from small children to brilliant professionals who simply haven't encountered this information in the same way that you have—you will have gained invaluable tools for handling conflict.

All turmoil has the potential to narrow vision and limit a person's ability to see anything other than the immediate trouble at hand. When that happens, either people don't have the kind of information that can help them handle the situation well, or they forget to apply what they do know. For example, imagine that you tell someone his shoe is untied, and he snaps back with, "I know how to tie my shoe!" He continues on his way without tying it and then a few steps later trips on the untied shoestring. In reality, he might very well know how to tie his shoe, but his actions demonstrate that he is not implementing his knowledge. Again, there could be many reasons why he's choosing not to tie his shoe, but the point here is that knowing information and applying it are two separate matters.

When you handle anger and conflict, it's essential for you to have insight regarding what might be happening on an individual psychological level, as well as what might be going on interpersonally in the potential dynamics of the situation. Your wider, outside-the-cave vision involves, at least in part, you keeping the following concepts in your foreground, as well as being able to apply them to your own life.

Expectations Versus Reality

▶ The shadow once said to the body, "You will never find another friend as valuable as me. Whether in sunlight or in moonlight, I follow you wherever you go."

And the body replied, "I do appreciate that you're with me in the light of the sun and the moon, but where do you go in the darkness, when I need you most?" ◀

If the body expected the shadow to follow her into the darkness, she would be let down when the shadow didn't show up; but if she aligned her expectations with the reality that her shadow either wasn't able or wasn't willing to be with her in times of darkness, then she would be less disappointed when her shadow didn't show up. That is why an essential part of both handling conflict and teaching others how to get through conflict centers on understanding how to align your expectations with reality.

The more you expect others to act in ways that you want them to act, the more disappointed you'll be. Remember, your cartoon-world view comprises what you think the world "should" be, not what the world actually is. Since you alone are in control of your expectations, the onus is on you to align your expectations with reality, rather than demanding that others be different from how they are. The more you can align your expectations with reality, the more prepared you'll be to respond to what is happening, instead of what you believe "should" be happening.

Beginning, Middle, End

No matter how angry, scared, anxious, sad, overwhelmed, or even happy you ever feel, every emotional experience has a beginning, a middle, and an end. In terms of conflict, that means that no matter how bad things are, eventually they will change. Of course, the grip of anger often leads us to believe that the cause of what we're feeling is, as Macbeth said, "the be-all and the end-all." It's essential, however, to know that every emotional experience will pass. And knowing that—not just intellectually but as a felt knowledge—is a profound gain, because when we are aware of the finiteness of our emotions, we can avoid making rash decisions in the beginning or middle of such emotions that will inevitably lead to worse endings.

In neurological terms, moments when you are cognitively aware that emotional experiences have a limited life-span center your brain in the higher-level thinking regions. Even if it's only a brief shift, taking the edge off a tough emotional moment, this cognitive awareness moves you out of the reactive, protective survival centers triggered by the fight-or-flight response. In other words, when you acknowledge intellectually that anger will eventually end, you soften the intensity of it. The analogy I like to use is adding an ice cube to hot tea: A single ice cube might not instantly cool the liquid off, but it does make it less scorching, which makes taking the first sip more manageable. Taking any heat off conflict helps move you toward the goal of getting through the conflict and ultimately learning from it. Recognizing that anger and conflict will pass through a beginning, a middle, and an end will not in and of itself cool the entirety of the feelings, but it will certainly help infuse the situation with hope as you approach it with the bigger picture in mind.

Your Mind Always Wants to Match Your Body

Here is an awakening piece of wisdom that can radically transform both the way you handle your own anger and the way you shine light on others' anger: Your mind always wants to match your body. In other words, however your body feels physically, your mind will race to create a narrative that makes sense out of why your body feels the way it does. For example, if you downed three energy drinks back to back, your body would mimic physiological anxiety. With a racing heart and body that feels physiologically anxious, your mind will search for the first possible reason it can find to explain why you might be feeling this way, and the rationale "I just had too much caffeine" would not likely be your mind's answer. Instead, you might think, "Oh, no, I forgot to . . ." or "I can't believe she said or did . . ." or something along those lines. Or perhaps you would think of a recent conflict that you didn't feel entirely settled around, and you would start playing that conflict over and over in your mind. Your mind would literally create a story to match how your body was feeling.

Understanding this mind-body link will prevent you from creating conflict-producing narratives. If you become aware that your mind always wants to match your body, you will be able to avoid the kind of emotional pitfalls that attach themselves to your extreme internal stories.

People See Actions, Not Intentions

When you hurt others unintentionally, it's natural for you to see your actions in light of your good intentions, but the reality is: People see only your actions, not your intentions. It's natural, too, to judge others solely by their actions, whereas you judge yourself by your intentions. Because it's natural for us to see our actions in light of our intentions and not to see others' intentions behind their actions, we have a tendency to minimize the pain we cause others and maximize the pain they cause us.

Minimizing the pain we cause involves using language that frames actions in acceptable ways. We use words like "just" and "only" to soften the reality of our actions. "I just raised my voice a little" sounds more tolerable than "I was screaming out of control." Regardless of how we choose to describe what we do, however, our actions speak for themselves.

An inmate in a maximum-security prison, whom I'll call "Dave," approached me to complain about his "unfair" prison sentence. I had just run a group he'd participated in, and he came up to me to talk one-on-one afterward.

> **Dave:** "Man, Doc, they got me up in here for not making a truck payment."

> **Me:** "Wait. Please say that again, because I really want to understand."

> **Dave:** "I'm telling you, they got me in here for not making a truck payment."

> **Me (in a lighthearted way):** "That's messed up. Honestly, I feel like I should pause this conversation and go call my wife; because if it's true that they can give you a state bid for missing a single payment, that's just scary . . ."

After we talked for a bit and he truly saw that I would never judge him for his actions, he felt safe enough to open up to me. That's when his defensiveness broke way into a smile and then a laugh. Checking to see that no one else was around, he then disclosed a more complete version of his story (that is, he showed me another side of the box): He'd gotten high on crystal meth and stolen a big rig. So technically they did arrest him for "not making a truck payment." He never made a payment because he'd hot-wired the truck and made off with it.

As comical as this true story is—and even Dave was able to laugh about the way he minimized what he did—it really exemplifies the concept of minimizing. Regardless of how any of us might attempt to soften our harsh actions with our descriptions, at the end of the day, what we did, we did, and the same is true of everyone else.

Extreme Language Produces Extreme Emotions

Think about a lemon. Don't go grab one for real, but just imagine it. Really picture it. See the yellow color it has. Feel its texture in your mind. Visualize holding that lemon in your hands and see yourself ripping that lemon apart. See the juices fly out of it. Now bring that lemon up to your mouth and take a big bite out of it. Can you imagine it? Did your mouth pucker at all? If it did, then consider how powerful this is: Words that you said in your mind produced an actual physiological response in your body.

Understanding that abstract words have a physical effect is crucial, especially when it comes to anger. Acknowledging that words have an impact is especially important when we realize that we all talk to ourselves, and our self-talk is ongoing throughout the day. In fact, the default-mode network is our running internal dialogue, which is estimated to consist of anywhere between 50,000 and 70,000 thoughts a day.

Research from the field of cognitive behavioral psychology has long demonstrated that what we tell ourselves significantly affects how we feel. When it comes to self-talk, extreme language is the biggest instigator of anger and conflict. If you run into an unexpected traffic jam and you say to yourself, "This is *terrible*! This *shouldn't* be happening! I *can't stand* this!" then you are likely going to feel pretty upset. The problem with using extreme words, or *catastrophizing*, is that it elicits a stronger reaction from us than the situation warrants. (Catastrophizing, or creating a catastrophe where one doesn't exist, is essentially making a mountain out of a molehill.) Perhaps more eye-opening, however, is the reality that extreme language is simply not accurate. Here's what actually occurs when we use extreme language: An event happens, we lie to ourselves, and then we make ourselves unnecessarily angry or upset. What if we were to look at the unexpected traffic jam above through the lens of accurate language? You might say to yourself something like, "This is *unfortunate*. I *wish* this wasn't happening right now, but *it's not the end of the world*, and I *can* handle it." The event stays the same, but how you feel about it and, ultimately, how you handle it shift.

The basic rule of language is that words mean something. The word "terrible," for instance, means "extremely bad or severe." Whereas it's true that an unexpected traffic jam is unfortunate, it is less true that it is extremely bad or severe. By telling yourself something that's not true, you respond much more intensely than the situation warrants. Conversely, it is true that the situation is unfortunate, but unfortunate situations do not require an extreme response or action from you.

Let's break down the second sentence, "This *shouldn't* be happening!" As we have seen, anytime we rely on the word "should," we are talking about the cartoon world, because in the real world the traffic jam is actually happening. Again, the world is not letting you down or deliberately angering you in that instance; only your perspective is doing that. When, by using extreme language, you back yourself into a psychological corner in your cartoon world, the only way out of it is through more extremes. So if you tell yourself something "*shouldn't* be happening" and it is, it makes sense that you feel you "*can't stand* it!" But that cartoon-world reality is simply is not true, either—in the real world you *are* standing it.

The more accurate statement "I wish this wasn't happening right now" is not only true, but it helps you set a healthy mental framework. From the time you were very young, you learned that wishes rarely come true. You might indeed wish that the traffic jam wasn't happening in that moment, but you might also wish for a billion dollars. You are getting neither of those wishes in the moment. But it is also true that it's not the end of the world, and you most certainly *can* handle it (as evidenced by the fact that you actually are).

When people rely on extreme language to describe their experience of the world, they also elicit extreme reactions from others. Be mindful of the hyperbole you use. In fact, be mindful of all your speech, because even if no one else is listening, you are. That is: You are listening to your own self-talk.

Here is a list of a few extreme words that can elicit extreme emotions:

- Always

- Never

- Everybody

- Nobody

- Can't stand it

Each of those words is rarely literally true, yet they have the power to flood your body with more cortisol and adrenaline than most situations typically warrant. Instead of using extreme language to describe your world or the conflicts you encounter, do your best to use more balanced, accurate adjectives. Remember, the cartoon world is filled with "shoulds" and extremes and magical thinking; the real world is the reality that is right at hand. The more accurate your language, the more you are grounded in the real world, and the less unnecessary intensity you add to situations.

Try this: Without censoring yourself in any way, write down a description of a recent conflict you experienced. Use as many adjectives as come to mind, including extreme words if they are a natural part of your vernacular in such situations. After you're finished, step away for a few minutes. Then, repeat the exercise, except this time describe the same situation without using any adjectives. Finally, take some time to read both descriptions of the conflict that you wrote down and observe your emotional reactions to each.

We Can Get Angry Without Knowing Why

Sometimes anger arises without us understanding where it comes from or why it's there. Sometimes we get angry to avoid feeling shame, depression, or anxiety. I've found that it can be incredibly freeing for people to begin to understand why they might be feeling the way that they are. In his book *Power vs. Force*, Dr. David Hawkins discusses what he calls a "map of consciousness," which can be used as a tool to show people how their thoughts contribute to how they feel. The map he created is one of my favorite mechanisms for helping people understand unconscious anger. I shortened it to five parts to create a scale of consciousness, as follows:

Knowledge/Compassion/Love
Anger
Anxiety
Depression
Shame

I call it a "scale" because it shows a general outline of basic levels of consciousness, or awareness. As you can see, at the bottom of the scale is shame. Shame is the lowest form of consciousness because it essentially amounts to people being aware enough to understand themselves as conscious beings but believing they are not worth anything. (Sometimes shame is conflated with guilt, but there is a distinction: With guilt, you might feel bad about what you do, whereas with shame, you feel bad about who you are.) As my own research and clinical experience has taught me over the last twenty years, people who live in shame act out of shame. In other words, if people feel worthless, there is very little to stop them from harming others. When people feel they are of little to no value, they tend to be unable to see or care about the value of others.

Right above shame on the scale is depression. When people are living in depression, they tend to live focused on the past and on their losses. Of course, clinical depression is also the result of chemical reactions in the brain, such as a lack of dopamine and serotonin, but just as the mind always wants to match the body, when the body feels physiologically sad, the mind tends to create a story to match it. In the case of depression, that story usually tends to center on the past.

Next up on the scale is anxiety. Neurologically, anxiety looks like fear. When you're anxious, your brain is sending excess cortisol throughout your body to keep you in a state of constant alertness. Cognitively, people experiencing anxiety tend to focus on the future. The fear is usually centered on what "might happen." Regardless of where a person's thoughts go with physiological anxiety, just like in depression, there is also a physical, neurological component to what they are experiencing. At a minimum, that feeling is uncomfortable. At a maximum, as with shame and depression, it can lead to extreme self-harm and even death.

The fascinating part of the scale of consciousness comes next. You will notice on the scale that anger is above shame, depression, and anxiety. Now, to be clear, knowledge and all the positive emotions, like compassion and love, are above anger, but the startling reality is that *anger is a higher form of consciousness than shame, depression, or anxiety.* There is neurological evidence for this. The chemical makeup of shame, depression, and anxiety involves a shortage of neurotransmitters like serotonin and dopamine and an excess of cortisol, none of which feels good. Interestingly, though, when we lash out in anger, our body releases endorphins, the so-called feel-good chemicals that are typically released anytime we engage in physical activity. Endorphin release is the reason that if you get hurt, you yell. When you're angry and lash out, you release endorphins, and you temporarily experience relief. Neurologically, we would rather be releasing endorphins than sitting in excess cortisol or suffering with a deficiency of serotonin or dopamine. This scale helps us make sense of why we sometimes get angry without knowing the reason. Anger carries us away from shame, depression, and anxiety.

Of course, that fact comes with a caveat. Just because it might make us temporarily feel better to escape shame, depression, or anxiety by lashing out in anger, that doesn't mean we *should* lash out. In fact, when we do, we often find ourselves feeling bad about it, which increases our sense of shame, which begins or perpetuates what I call "the cycle of shame." Without conscious education about this unhealthy cycle, people can continuously live out this behavioral pattern for a long time. The key to breaking free from the cycle of shame is to utilize the states of consciousness that exist above those first four. Knowledge provides the awareness of what's happening. Compassion allows people to be easy on themselves when they are feeling shame, depression, or anxiety, which ultimately can lead to them talking about what's occurring inside them in a healthy way. And love is the pinnacle: At our best, we are kind, caring, and compassionate.

The Transactional Dynamics of Conflict

Conscious education isn't just about you understanding what's occurring on an individual psychological level. It also involves you having a sense of how basic interpersonal dynamics tend to play out. To understand the dynamics of conflict, it's important to develop a bird's-eye view of the impact you have on others and how they, in turn, impact you.

You play a role in every interaction you have. Your every action elicits a reaction in others. Although we are all responsible solely for what we do in life, it would be unrealistic to deny that our actions influence others and vice versa. In other words, you don't *cause* others to act in a specific way (or they, you), but your actions do influence others' reactions, just as theirs influence yours. Since you experience your role through a first-person perspective, it's difficult to see how you're affecting others in the moment. The more skilled you become at identifying people's behavioral patterns while they're occurring, the more effectively you will be able to alter what you're doing to affect what others do right then and there. Knowing this pattern will radically shift the way you handle conflict.

In the late 1950s, a psychiatrist named Eric Berne conceived a model of human interactions that he called "transactional analysis." Transactional analysis (TA) might sound intimidating, but "trans" just means "across," and "actions" are behaviors, and "analysis" is to evaluate something, so transactional analysis is simply a method of evaluating the way people interact.

TA is centered on the idea that communication can almost be seen as a game. (In fact, in 1964 Berne wrote a book called *Games People Play*, which became a major best seller.) That is, you learned long ago that when you act one way, others respond accordingly, and when you act a different way, their responses change. We play games to get what we want, not because we're wrong or bad or inherently manipulative, but because we've learned somewhere along the way that people respond to each other in fairly predictable patterns. Furthermore, according to Berne, everyone lives out of what he calls three "ego states": Parent, Adult, and Child.

The Parent ego state is split into the Nurturing Parent and the Critical Parent. As its name implies, the Nurturing Parent is the part of you that's loving, kind, and compassionate; it's the caretaker in you. The Critical Parent, on the other hand, is, as its name indicates, the critical, demanding part of you that insists others be how you deem they "should" be (that is, according to your cartoon-world view).

The Child ego state is split into two parts as well. The Fun Child is the part of you that wants to be carefree, laugh, joke, play around, and have fun. The Hurt Child is the "poor me" aspect of you that is ever the victim and for whom nothing is ever enough.

The Adult ego state is the rational, logical part of you. Your Adult regulates all the other ego states, and when the Adult does not check the other states, we tend to suffer. For example, if your Nurturing Parent state is too active, without the Adult to regulate it, you will likely find yourself being taken advantage of by or enabling others. If you have too much Critical Parent without the Adult to balance it, you're just mean and toxic to be around. Too much Fun Child without enough Adult, and you are highly irresponsible. Too much Hurt Child without the Adult, and you become the insufferably helpless victim who is draining to others. You need the Adult to anchor and balance you, and when you have it, you can effectively share the best aspects of your Nurturing Parent and Fun Child with others.

The Critical Parent ego state tends to play the biggest role in conflict. The Critical Parent brings out either the Hurt Child or the Critical Parent in others. If it elicits the Hurt Child, the result can be a seemingly endless drama of blame and victimhood. The Critical Parent might say something to the effect of, "You shouldn't have done . . . ," to which the Hurt Child replies, "You don't understand how hard it is for me . . ." and the two of them struggle to be able to listen to each other, much less reach consensus. But some of the highest levels of conflict arise when one person's Critical Parent brings out the Critical Parent in others. A Critical Parent to Critical Parent interaction often consists of two people going back and forth in a manner that escalates: I fire at you, and you fire back at me, in an ever-intensifying spiral. Critical Parent to Critical Parent is a content-to-content interaction, in which I say, "You are a . . . ," and you say, "Well, you are a . . . " From a position of Critical Parent, neither of us makes the effort to genuinely listen to or validate the other.

I include TA in this "Essential Wisdom" section not only to give you an easily understandable model of human dynamics but also to help you see that one of the best ways you can ever handle anger and conflict is by staying in your Adult ego state, regardless of what ego state others are in. Staying in the Adult means maintaining control of yourself and not being reactive. It's not going up with other people's anger highs or down with their self-pity lows. When you learn to stay in your Adult consistently, you will find yourself remaining clear and effective regardless of how out of control others might be.

Be the Couch

Imagine there's a couch against a wall, and you throw a rubber ball into the couch. It stays there, right? So if you want to throw the ball again, you have to walk all the way over, pick it up, walk all the way back, and then throw it again. Eventually, you'd get tired and stop throwing the ball.

Essentially, I teach people to "be the couch" when handling conflict. When you're the couch (or when you're in your Adult ego state), you don't fire back at others, and eventually they lose steam and stop sending negative energy your way. Quite literally what this looks like is you responding to others' process by validating them rather than getting caught up in the content of what they say. As others lose the energy of their anger, you are able to help them pull out their Adult.

The most effective way to be the couch and stay in your Adult is to listen and validate others. Once others feel validated, they are able to move into their own Adult ego state. In an Adult to Adult interaction, the focus is more on exploring options than on expressing emotions. The more you are able to stay in your Adult ego state, the more you will be able to bring out the Adult in others.

Imagine your coworker accuses you of doing something you haven't done. Imagine this person accosts you and is visibly enraged. The more defensive you become, the more you make yourself the solid wall against which the person can keep firing, which only escalates the conflict. If, instead, you can validate the person's anger (using language like "Sounds like you're really angry" or "It seems like you're pretty convinced it was me who did that") without being attached or defensive, the more you are the couch, and the less that person has to react against. Your ego will likely want you to rise to the Critical Parent level and defend yourself ("I didn't say that!"), or your Hurt Child might want to sulk ("It's not fair that you're accusing me")—both perspectives are from a cartoon-world belief that the person "shouldn't" be accusing you, but the reality is that they are, and all you can do is work from this moment forward. Transactional analysis can be an incredibly empowering tool to help you identify both how others affect you and how you affect others, so that you can operate from your Adult. The more focused you stay on process, from your Adult, the faster the other person in the conflict will de-escalate and be able find their own Adult.

Counterfactual Thinking

In addition to your cartoon-world mind inundating you with all the "shoulds" that you believe "need" to be happening, there is another, even deeper way that your mind attempts to convince you that you have control over reality. *Counterfactual thinking* is comprised of the "If . . . then" statements we use to give ourselves the illusion that we have more control than we do. Counterfactuals help people mentally undo events or create an alternative reality. Sometimes we use counterfactuals to imagine a better outcome than the one that occurred: "If I had insisted that my son not play football, then he wouldn't have gotten into that car accident on his way to practice." We also use counterfactuals to consider how things might have been worse: "If I had taken that higher paying job, then I might have been on that plane that was in an accident, so it's a good thing I didn't take the job." Counterfactuals either help us feel like we have more control than we actually do or help us confirm what we cannot change.

Understanding counterfactual thinking is important because doing so helps us see how we create fictitious realities and then base actual emotions on them. When it comes to anger and conflict management, all too often people attempt to attribute control where control doesn't exist. Understanding counterfactuals allows you to meet people where they are, discern their logic, and lead them in a way that helps them direct themselves down the path that's best for them. It also helps you walk through your own anger in the most conscious way possible. In addition, counterfactual thinking can skew the way you explore options with others, so it's vital to be aware of the way it impacts decision-making, both when you're exploring options that have already been made and when you're looking at future options.

Doubt Your Assumptions

Whereas counterfactuals take what's already happened and create an "If . . . then" consequential perspective, assumptions are essentially proactive "If . . . then" ideas: "If we work together, we can bring down this mammoth," or "If we try this, we might get this result." Every risk, small or large, is predicated on an assumption, even if that assumption occurs below our conscious awareness.

My guess is that it was evolutionarily advantageous for us to make assumptions. The human intellect has made it possible for us to succeed on a planet where we are not the strongest, fastest, biggest, or most physically capable. We succeeded as a species in many ways thanks not just to our ability to evaluate completed actions and see what happened (that is, learning through stimulus response), but also because of our ability to make assumptions about what might happen.

Risks predicated on assumptions helped us survive; but the dark underside of risk is failure, and the reality is that assumptions do not always work out. When it comes to conflict, making assumptions often gets you into more trouble than not. The key factor to avoiding unnecessary, assumption-driven anger is doubt, which gives you the ability to say, "Maybe I don't see the whole picture." Doubting your assumptions does two important things. First, it grants you a moment to pause and rein in impulsive reactions. Second, it adds an element of uncertainty that can soften your anger. But it's important to avoid confusing doubting your assumptions with any other kind of doubt (such as doubting your abilities). Doubting your assumptions applies only to you taking a moment to realize that you might not be seeing all the sides of the proverbial box. The more you can do that up front, the less likely you'll be to react angrily

In the Tao Te Ching, Lao Tzu wrote, "The ancient Masters didn't try to educate the people, but kindly taught them to not-know." This statement might seem contradictory, but in Taoism "not-knowing" is a sign of wisdom, much different from the confident "knowing" assumptions of the ego. Lao Tzu also wrote, "When they think that they know the answers, people are difficult to guide. When they know that they don't know, people can find their own way." Doubting your own certainty, as well as helping people doubt theirs, is one of the most useful ways to de-escalate conflict and walk directly through anger.

Understanding Crisis-Prone People

Imagine a scale from 1 to 10, with 1 being the baseline of a normal-functioning brain and 10 being the brain experiencing a high crisis. Crisis-prone people's brains regularly operate at a high point in the scale, and they often resort to conflict because they don't know a better way to deal with what is happening inside of them. As you've seen, it's natural for your mind to want to match your body, so if your body feels chemically off or physically anxious, for example, your mind will race to make up a story to match how you feel. When you look at the baseline of a normal-functioning brain, you see that it doesn't operate as if it's in a crisis.

Notice that my description is a "normal-functioning brain" and makes no reference to a person being "normal" or not. This is only a descriptor of the way the human brain normally develops. Although we are hard-wired to take in and ultimately handle crises, the normal development of the human brain takes longer than brain development in many other species. Infants and toddlers, for example, are naturally dependent on others to handle their safety. When people experience a trauma, however, their brain circuitry rewires to be ready for any kind of crisis at any time. This is what I would call a *crisis-prone individual*: a person whose brain already feels as if it's in crisis and who is ready to see a crisis in any situation.

Because crisis-prone people's amygdalae tend to be on higher alert than normal-functioning brains (usually because they have endured trauma), they tend to feel as if they are in crisis more frequently. Feeling physiologically in crisis (from excess cortisol and adrenaline), crisis-prone people have a tendency to create crises around them to make sense of how they feel. It's not that crisis-prone people enjoy being in crisis situations; rather, it's that being in an actual crisis makes the most sense for them (because their minds are racing to match their body). Until, of course, they learn a more conscious way of handling their physiological emotions (for example, through mindfulness, emotion regulation, or other techniques).

If you find that you have a tendency to "create problems" where none exist, you might be struggling with crisis-prone tendencies. Learning to avoid creating a story is paramount to dealing with the kind of anxiety that your brain vibrating at a 4 or a 5 can bring. If, conversely, you find yourself encountering crisis-prone individuals, then it's extremely important to be mindful of what might be occurring with them. The more you recognize that the person feels in crisis, the less you have to take that crisis personally, and the more you can focus on being the couch, for example, and reflecting process far more than content. In either case, knowledge is power—or, perhaps more accurately, knowledge is a pathway to peace.

Summary

Conscious education is about moving people from emotion to reason at the speed of insight. There is a difference between intellectually recognizing psychological concepts and practicing them in your everyday life. The more you practice living in accord with the wisdom that you understand intellectually, the easier it will be to share information with others in ways that inspire them to want to listen to what you have to offer. Conscious education helps widen people's perspective on life by adding meaningful insight. Since anger and conflict tend to narrow our vision, conscious education—widening what we see—is especially important in times of conflict and difficult emotional experiences.

> Anger has no arms or legs; it is neither courageous
> nor clever; how then, has it reduced me to its slave?
> **SHANTIDEVA**

Creativity

Beyond One-Size-Fits-All Problem Solving

Creativity can be your friend or your enemy when it comes to anger. As your friend, creativity can help you find unique ways to meet others where they are and move them through anger in the quickest way possible. Creativity can also help you make adventures out of every obstacle you encounter. As your enemy, creativity can add overwhelming, untrue, and unnecessary dialogue to your internal thoughts, causing you to generate significantly more anger than any given situation warrants. Creativity can come in the form of a narrative that either gives meaning or purpose to even the most intense conflict or magnifies even the smallest bump in the road. When you learn to understand and tap into creativity, you give yourself a path to peace, and you can provide the same for others as well.

As we've seen throughout this book, Yield Theory is predicated on meeting people where they are and helping them move from emotion to intellect. It's growth focused: The intended end result is to learn from every interaction. Whereas conscious education is centered on learning about and then offering information that awakens insight, the fundamental component of creativity emphasizes delivering that information in unique ways that consider different people's individual needs. Even under normal conditions, people learn in diverse ways. In the heat of conflict, however, when people are operating out of defensiveness and emotion, sparking the kind of insight that resonates with them in ways that target their higher-level decision-making processes becomes even more challenging. In this chapter, I'll show you how to use creativity as your friend to help you handle your own emotions, as well as to help you elicit others' desire to learn, even in the midst of anger and conflict. I'll also show you how to be mindful of creativity as an enemy that builds needless conflict and angst.

Anger locks us into one-track minds. In the throes of anger, even trying to consider other options can be tough, but creativity is the ever-present instrument that can redirect attention from its current course. In moments of conflict, sometimes all you need to be able to do is introduce an idea long enough for other areas of the brain to rush in and reinforce that something besides the impulsive and grippingly angry thought is possible. Allowing even one additional idea in gives our minds the option of at least two tracks to operate on, and then, of course, the door opens for other paths of action as well.

Creativity likely played a role in the survival of our species. If our prelinguistic ancestors couldn't go toe-to-toe with or outrun potential predators, they had to find inventive ways to hide (from climbing trees to crouching in caves to eventually building shelters) or fight (creating weapons, whether for defending or for hunting). Our species' fight-flight-freeze amygdalae evolved to work in conjunction with our more advanced cognitive functioning to help our early ancestors rely on creativity to handle conflict. Many millennia after the first of our kind, creativity remains one of our biggest assets for handling conflict, walking through anger, and dealing with our most challenging situations.

Creativity might have begun as a survival asset, but the impact it's had on our infinitely vast internal psychological worlds is that it has given us the ability to self-actualize and thrive. From technology to art to finding solutions to conflict, being creative is one of the most beautiful and helpful expressions of our humanity. Unfortunately, its dark underbelly is that it is also the source of some of our most intense psychological pain, neuroses, and ugliest conflicts. Without an awareness of how creativity manifests in different narratives, we can easily create unnecessary suffering and conflict. Difficult as it might be to realize, all of us have created an immense amount of unnecessary suffering in our lives. As we have seen, your mind always want to match your body, and when your body is feeling off, your mind will race to create a story to make sense of why you are feeling that way. Every time your mind seeks to match your unsettled body by delivering a false narrative that detracts from you getting to the actual origin of your physiological feelings, your self-talk is toxic. Beyond the immediate mind-wanting-to-match-your-body phenomenon, however, you also create long-standing narratives from which you establish your world view.

Creativity as Enemy

When we are experiencing anxiety, sometimes the more creative we are, the more creativity becomes our enemy, because it pushes us to run with fear-induced thoughts, and the distance we take those thoughts is more a reflection of our creativity rather than of actuality. For example, if a random thought about your relationship partner being interested in someone else pops into your mind and your body already feels physiologically anxious, then you are likely to run with that thought in creative ways. As the anxiety you feel moves up the scale of consciousness to anger, what began as a random, impulsive thought can turn into an outright conflict with your loved one. "Why would you like that person?!" you might demand from your partner, who wonders where the heck your anger is originating from, because they couldn't see how anxiety moved to jealousy in your mind.

Whatever your long-term narratives are, your short-term narratives are likely to support. If your long-standing narrative, for instance, is that you do not see yourself as worthy of others' love, then the short-term stories you create in your mind will race to support that view. Worse, your creative brain will rely on confirmation bias to find what you're looking to see.

Creativity can lead you to create a vast internal cartoon world that continuously sets you up for conflict. The "shoulds" you demand of the world aren't reality—they're a creative fiction that, as you've seen throughout this book, can damage relationships, interfere with your peace, and lead to unnecessary anger if left unchecked. The use of hyperbole, for instance, can make situations instantly more volatile than they need to be. Imagine a teenager screaming to her friend, "I can't stand you anymore!" The more accurate statement, after all, is that she *can* stand the other person, but she might be annoyed or put off by something that person said or did. Her brain, however, interprets her own "I can't stand it" as an intense threat to herself, which translates to a more extreme reaction than the situation warrants. This is, in effect, how creativity contributes to anger and conflict. Creativity can be harmful to all of us when we don't recognize the ways in which it can make mountains out of molehills; but outside of fictitious narratives, creativity can be a trusted and powerful ally.

Creativity as Friend

As a problem solver, your creativity is one of the biggest strengths you can rely on for handling anger and conflict. Imagine being angry and then tapping into your creative self to redefine anything you're experiencing. For example, the next time you encounter people or situations that are functioning at a significantly slower pace than you wish they would, try seeing them as intentionally placed mental exercise equipment that is solely designed to help you build your muscle of patience. "Oh, thank you for cutting me off—what a great opportunity for me to get better at increasing my self-control." Tapping into your creativity gives you endless ways to view everything you encounter as a purposeful part of the story of your life. How you write your role in that moment is, of course, entirely up to you.

One day I was driving down the road and found myself consumed with angry thoughts. I didn't like the feeling of anger that was flowing through me, so I imagined my anger personified as a wise man sitting in the passenger seat next to me. I then had a conversation with my anger. I asked him what he was doing there, what he was looking for from me, and how long he planned to stay. By detaching myself from my feeling and creating a dialogue with my now personified emotion, I was able to quickly move from my reactive experience of anger in that moment to an insightful, intellectual understanding of what I was feeling. In so doing, I was able to release that anger (I even visualized that, at a red light, he got out and went on his way).

Using your creativity to shift what you're experiencing is powerful and freeing. And there are endless ways for you to tap into creativity to gain insight and awareness, including experiential exercises, metaphors, analogies, and teaching tales. Using creativity as an integral tool for your own personal growth is enlightening, but my emphasis on creativity doesn't end there. Creativity is one of the seven fundamental components of Yield Theory because drawing on creativity to help others move through their experience of anger and conflict is transformative. I've spent a career using creative metaphors and techniques to help bring awareness to others and initiate an internal motivation for them to move through their anger and conflict. In the next section, I'll show you some of the most helpful creative techniques you can use to bring about insight for angry people. Because teaching tales are essential to Yield Theory and integral to my personal method for using creativity to spark conscious education in others, I've also included an appendix of additional teaching tales at the end of this book.

Don't Be a Puppet!

One of the most creative metaphors to help elicit awareness in others is what I call my "puppet technique." Just as a marionette is controlled by a puppet master who moves the puppet this way and that, so, too, are you and I behaving like a puppet anytime we allow others to determine what we think about or how we feel. Let's say, for instance, that you're going about your day feeling fine, when all of a sudden someone says or does something that alters the course of your thoughts, feelings, or mood. In that instance, you allowed that person to control you. Without realizing it, you permitted her to be your puppet master. When you recognize that you are willingly giving people the reins to control what you think, how you feel, or what you do, it sparks a rebellious, naturally defensive part of you that is not comfortable with freely giving control of your life over to others.

For many angry people who thrive on communicating how tough they are, the metaphor of the puppet is eye-opening. If you're talking to someone who is furious that others "disrespected" him, for example, offering the puppet metaphor can transform his perspective. You could say, "So you're telling me you willingly give others the power to make you upset?" or "So all anyone who wants to control you like a puppet has to do is say the right combination of words, and then they'll be in complete control of what you think, how you feel, and what you do?" Creatively applying the puppet metaphor in a conflict moves people's desire to be in control of their own life into the foreground of the conversation, and it does so in a way that doesn't put any psychological objects between you and that person. In other words, it's entirely an internal dilemma for a person to work out: Do they actually want to willingly give others control? Or not want to give others control? By offering the puppet metaphor, you internally motivate people to consciously take control of their lives. The instant any of us realizes that we do not want to be other people's puppet is the moment we become more open to learning about the ways in which we can actually cut the strings.

Keep Your Power

We all have an innate power that drives our lives. Our power source moves us forward in life, allowing us to reach our full potential. Unfortunately, our power is intangible. I say "unfortunately," because I believe if our power was tangible—that is, if we could see it and feel it—then we could better protect it, and we would be significantly less likely to give that power away. In Marvel Comics, the hero Iron Man provides a great visual of this concept. Iron Man wears a suit of armor that's powered by a visible power source on his chest. Just as you would not expect to see this superhero take off his power source and hand it to whomever he's battling, it's equally important for you to hold on to your power in times of conflict.

Just as it's a fact that the sun shines during the day, not the night, it's a fact that when you are reactive to others, you are giving them your power. So if someone cuts you off in traffic and you get angry, you have given that person your power. If someone says something and you ruminate on it, allowing him to "rent space" in your mind and causing yourself angst, you have given that person your power. If a person does something that you didn't want her to do or don't agree with and you allow that person's actions to determine your inner experience of life, you have given that person your power.

Try this: Pick up an object near you that you can hold easily in one hand (a water bottle, a phone, a bookmark—anything that's immediately accessible and that you can hold). Now imagine that the object you picked up represents your power source. Maybe even hold the object close to your chest to mimic Iron Man. Now I want you to imagine that someone comes by and says or does something unkind to you. The moment you hear the unkind words, do you think it's wise to hand your power source over to the person who's being mean to you? Are you really willing to take off your power source and hand it to others? It seems a bit ridiculous, in this context, to think about giving away your power to anyone, let alone to someone who is mean to you.

I often use this technique as a direct way to confront others about being readily willing to give away their power, and I don't only bring it up in a clinical setting. I use it as a creative way to bring about awareness in anyone I talk to in life who is genuinely giving away their power. When you share a visual like this with others, it shows you are striking together *with* them to handle the conflict they're experiencing. Helping people see how easily they're giving away their power, as well as giving them insight into how they can stop doing so, sparks awareness without eliciting defensiveness.

Although it's rarely comfortable to realize just how easily we give away our power, there's little arguing that the visual itself is awakening. As with any conscious information, it's important first to work on mastering not giving away your own power; as you do, others will be more receptive to you teaching them to do the same. The creative exercise of holding on to your power might seem simple to understand, but in practice, it can be absolutely profound.

A man in one of my anger management groups once told me that he saw a rival gang member who had stabbed him in the past walking down his street. The man in my group said, "I went inside to get my gun. But when I got my gun out and cocked it, I saw your face, Doc." So I said, "Oh, I have to hear more now." He explained, "When I cocked my gun, I remembered what you taught us about giving away our power. I realized right then and there that if I would have gone out and shot that guy, I would have given him my power, and I didn't want to do that. So I put the gun down, closed my front door, stayed inside, and I kept my power."

The creative metaphor of giving away power stuck with him in such a way that he was able to draw on and pragmatically use it in a real, and potentially serious, conflict. This technique has worked for me, as well as for countless people I've shared it with. I've found people are more likely to be receptive to hearing you when, in sharing the concept, you tap into the way you have also given away your power at times. This doesn't mean you necessarily have to share a specific experience, but you can convey authenticity with your tone so that the listener knows you, too, know the feeling of willingly giving away your power. Your vulnerability and openness elicits openness in return.

The puppet and the power metaphors form a cornerstone to Yield Theory, because both visuals force people into the mental paradox of their egos wanting them to be "right" but also very much not wanting to be controlled by others. The paradox elicits insight, and insight sparks change. My invitation is for you to sit with both the puppet and the power techniques and then begin to apply each of them to your life. The first time you encounter something that would have routinely upset you or elicited your anger, think about those instances in light of becoming someone else's puppet or giving away your power. The longer you sit with these ideas and the more you practice them, the more effectively you'll be able to draw on them in potentially volatile situations.

Relying on Instinct

In terms of sharing these and other techniques with others, my rule of thumb is that the simpler you can make creative explanations, the better. Remember, the goal in using creativity is to shift people away from their emotional center and into their higher-level thinking center. Simple analogies are like providing a short, sturdy, easy-to-cross bridge, whereas longer explanations are like having to cross an enormous chasm over a shaky walkway. The following is an example of a "short and sturdy" analogy that creatively provided the necessary segue for a man in crisis.

▶ A former athlete came to me with tremendous internal conflict and anger. He complained that he couldn't decide whether to stay in his current relationship. As he described his partner's repeated infidelity and constant belittling and hurtful treatment of him, mixed with his uncertainty of what he should do, I grabbed a soft stress ball from my desk. Without warning and without saying anything, I tossed it right at him. His reflexes kicked in, and his hands immediately sprang up to catch it. He smiled, seemingly caught off guard, and he looked at me with surprise. I asked, "Did you have to think about catching that?" He said, "No, I just did." I then asked, "Do you really not know what to do about this relationship?" He sat up, put his shoulders back, opened his eyes widely (as if awakening), and said, with confidence, "I shouldn't be in this relationship. It's not good for me at all." And so he made his decision. ◀

When conflict leads to people feeling lost or trapped in indecision, helping them rely on their instinct to guide them is a wise move. There were different ways I could have chosen to deliver that information, but I'm aware that creative experiential exercises tend to stick with people. In twenty-plus years, I cannot think of any instances when I actively planned ahead regarding which creative technique I might use. Instead, I trust as long as I'm fully present with people, at some point my own creative instinct will kick in when it's needed. So although I didn't set out to throw a stress ball at my client that day, in the moment, my gut told me it was the right way to spark insight.

By relying on your instinct, you too can apply creative experiential awareness exercises to the way you handle conflict. I say "relying on your instinct" because oftentimes I encounter people who tell me that they're "not creative." I disagree. The kind of creativity I'm talking about is inherently human. It takes practice to develop, but often the most limiting factor to developing creativity is negative self-talk. Either people will say that they're not creative, or they will worry that the creative solutions they come up with won't be well received. In either case, one of the best ways you can develop your creativity is by brainstorming solutions without judging whatever ideas come to mind.

Think of either a recent or current conflict, and then brainstorm as many different resolutions as you can. Play each one out in your mind. Be mindful not to judge, naysay, or limit resolutions. Since this is a mental exercise and no one is acting out what comes to your mind, there is no reason to stop yourself from running through any solutions that enter it. In other words, if building a rocket ship and flying off to Mars is a solution that pops into your mind, sit with it momentarily, play it out if you want, and then move on. The point is to tap into your most instinctual creativity and then to continue practicing tapping into it until you feel comfortable thinking of different ideas. The more you practice your creativity, the better you get at it. If you practice brainstorming creativity outside of emotional interactions, it becomes easier to draw upon creativity in new moments of conflict.

A Room-Temperature Hot Coal

One of my favorite gifts I received as a professor came from a group of counseling students I taught in graduate school. They gave me a T-shirt printed with a water bottle in the front and with what they called my "Conte-isms" arranged around the water bottle in a circle. The image came from the fact that, through the years, I tend to use the water bottle that I often have with me as my prop for different analogies and metaphors. For instance, in one moment the water bottle might be my "puppet," so I can do a physical demonstration with it. At another time, the water bottle might represent my "power source," so that I can show a visual of giving that power away. You, too, can use whatever objects are handy to illustrate a creative idea. Physical objects make abstract ideas tangible, and the more creative you are with them, the more memorable an insight you can offer to others.

One time a client of mine was consumed by anger toward a former friend. Even though she hadn't spoken to her former friend in some time and didn't even know where the woman was currently living, she allowed herself to expend an incredible amount of negative mental energy thinking about her. She said she was constantly ruminating over a way she could hurt the woman who obviously had hurt her. As I was listening to her describe what she felt like, a vision became very present to me: Buddha's saying that being angry is like picking up a hot coal to throw at someone else: it burns you before it ever gets to the other person. I wanted to demonstrate this point to her in a creative way that would make an impact and be memorable, so I grabbed my trusty water bottle and set it down next to her. I then shared the Buddha's metaphor of anger as a hot coal.

I asked her to imagine that the water bottle was a scorching hot coal, and then I invited her to pick it up so that she could visualize throwing it at her former friend. She smiled and willingly picked up the bottle to throw. I said, "Remember, it's scorching hot, so you're going to want to throw it quickly." She replied, "Well, then, where is she, so I can throw it already?"

"That's just it!" I said. "Every second you look around for where she is, you are the one suffering, not her. You are continually burning yourself, and the reality is: That's what your anger is doing to you. You're so fixated on your anger and hatred toward her that you're hurting yourself constantly as you wait to get her in your mind."

She put the water bottle down in a swift move, smiled briefly, and wrung her hands together as if to soothe them. I pointed at her action of putting the "hot coal" down and said enthusiastically, "That's it! You know instinctively that this anger is harming your peace, and you don't even want to hold an imaginary hot coal, so imagine what the very real thoughts of anger are burning into you and doing to you physically . . ." She became still, looked at the ground, then looked up and smiled. She had a cathartic release.

She said, "I see that I don't want to get her, but I do want to get rid of this anger." I said, "Now that, you can do!" And before long, she learned how to let go of the anger that had consumed so much of her mental space. The next time you find yourself consumed with anger, look around you: What objects can represent a burning coal to you?

It was creativity that led me to using a water bottle to represent the Buddha's point about picking up a hot coal and make it a tangible concept for her. Yield Theory helped me meet her where she was, not resist her anger, and even play out the option (in a safe environment) of what following through with trying to hurt her ex-friend might actually look like. The fundamental component of creativity inspired me to avoid telling her to stop thinking about her anger and, instead, to turn a powerful statement about what anger does to the angry person into an experiential technique.

You can turn the same technique on yourself. Picture how your anger toward someone else is like you holding that hot coal. And you ruminating about your anger toward that person is like you constantly burning yourself with that hot coal as you run around looking for the person at whom you want to throw it. Anger at others might drive you to want to be distanced from them; but the more mental energy you expend on others, even in anger, the more you are actually linked to them. Even clearly visualizing an experiential exercise like this can give you awareness about the effect your anger is having on you.

The Power of Storytelling

Creativity in Yield Theory can be manifested in myriad ways and is bound only by the limits of your own mind. It was important for me to include creativity as a fundamental component in this book because an inescapable reality is that people learn in different ways, and simply stating facts is not always the most effective way to share information. (It can even at times, as mentioned earlier, elicit the backfire effect.) One of the most powerful ways to use creativity in handling conflict is through storytelling. I have made a career out of using metaphors and teaching tales to help people shift from the emotional center of their brain to the thinking center in direct, nonthreatening ways. For me, telling brief stories is like putting highly enticing appetizers out at a party: People need no overt directive to both gravitate toward them and start eating. In the same way, when you offer stories in a nonattached, compassionate, and nondemanding way, you will find that your ideas become significantly more enticing than if you presented them in the abstract.

To use storytelling effectively, timing is vital, both in how you relate a tale and in when you choose to tell it. It's essential to learn the stories so well that you can tell them as if you were present when they occurred. In addition, it's important to be unattached to the way others receive or don't receive them. Stories are incredibly powerful precisely because there never is any one particular element that people "have" to get out of them. Instead, it's more important to assess what people actually *do* get from them or even what parts do not resonate with them. Assessing how others respond to stories gives you valuable information regarding where they are in their process of change.

Telling brief tales to de-escalate conflict works on several levels. First, a story redirects attention away from the current content and energy of the conflict. Second, we're hardwired to be drawn to storytelling, so people immediately move from talking to listening. Third, stories have layers, and people pick up on different aspects of stories at different times. The right story at the right time can tap into the emotional turmoil others are experiencing, and if they then sit with the aspects that evoke something in them, they can more easily lead themselves out of the turmoil. Again, observing which aspect of a story either resonates or doesn't with others, as well as assessing how others react to hearing the stories, provides great information regarding where people are in moving through the conflict.

Imagine your teenager comes home furious after school. He discloses that while he and his friends were joking around and making fun of one another, he felt they were picking on him more than he was dishing it back. As he talks to you, he gets angrier and angrier. You recognize that in his cartoon world, he likely believes his friends "shouldn't" have said anything in response to what he said or maybe even that he "should" have said other insults. Instead of telling him, "Just don't be so angry" (which is invalidating and minimizing), or even trying to logically explain to him that he seems to be taking the mutual joking more personally than the other boys (which would likely add to his defensiveness), you could offer him the following story.

"Give Me Your Legs!"

▶ Once a young, troubled monk went to the master and told him that he was being picked on by the other monks. The master sat in silence for a moment, as he wasn't sure if the young monk had finished speaking. The young monk became angry at the master's silence and said, "Oh, so you're taking their side now? I come to tell you that your students are picking on me, and you say nothing!" Taken aback by this young monk's quick anger, the master reflected another moment, but his silence made the young monk even angrier. "Oh, now you think you're so holy?! You think you're better than me? You think you're so great and wonderful, but your students pick on me, and you just take their side!"

The master finally spoke: "Give me your legs." The young monk was confused and thrown off. "What? You're not even listening to me! I'm telling you they really are picking on me!" The master repeated, a bit more forcefully, "Give me your legs!" The young monk was disturbed by this and confused still. "No!" he said. "I don't even know what you're talking about! I'm trying to tell you—" The master interrupted him midsentence and yelled out in anger, "Cut off your legs and give them to me now!" And the student, enraged at the thought of this, fired back, "No! No!"

Then the master said, "Why is it that you defend your body so fiercely, yet you give away your mind so easily?" In that moment the young monk understood. He never gave away his mind again. ◀

Your teenager, like the young monk in this tale, might also be equally quick to defend his body but give away his mind. Sharing a teaching tale like this does several things: First, it grabs his attention because it's an interesting story. Second, it shows your teenager that he's not alone (that is, others have felt like him before), but it doesn't express that in a way that diminishes his own, very real experience. Third, it captivates his frontal cortex (the thinking center) enough to shift energy at least temporarily away from his amygdala (fight-or-flight response). Finally, it gives the two of you a quick insight statement to refer to from here on out. The next time he goes to school, you can lightheartedly remind him not to "give away his legs."

Teaching Stories

Teaching stories like "Give Me Your Legs!" can offer a wellspring of insight for people. You can utilize them in ways that help you circumvent others' defensiveness and expand their awareness, even in the midst of conflict. Your own experience with these stories will play a role in how you deliver them. It's wise to be mindful that people derive their own meaning from stories, and you cannot force the same "ah-ha!" moments on others that you yourself might have had. All you can do is be aware of when and how you deliver the stories; the rest is up to the listener.

The following are three creative teaching tales that can elicit impactful change in others. (For many more teaching tales you can use, see appendix B.) One is a tale I heard, the second is one that I made up, and the third comes from my clinical experience. All of the stories I recount in this book are ones I invite you to integrate into your own life and then tell to others in a way that most suits you. The more you're able to make these stories a part of your own narrative, the more naturally you will be able to share them with others.

Two Monks

▶ A younger monk was accompanying an older monk on a journey. Along the way, they encountered a woman who was trying to cross a shallow river but did not want to get her dress wet. Without hesitation or uttering a word, the older monk picked up the woman and carried her across the river. He set her down on the other side, and he and the young monk continued on their way in silence.

About an hour after the event, the young monk turned to the older monk and said, "I can't believe you picked that woman up! We took a vow never to touch a woman, and you just walked right up to her and picked her up against your body!" The older monk simply replied, "Brother, I set her down an hour ago. Why are you still carrying her?" ◀

Think of the anger you've held onto over the years. Sure, you've naturally wanted others to forget the harm you've caused them, yet your ego convinced you that the slights you caused were okay and that it was likewise okay to hold onto the slights others committed against you.

Setting down your anger is significant because it helps you transcend your ego and live from your essence. The past already happened and is over, so the challenge you face now is accepting that. The more you practice setting down anything that harmed your ego in the past, the more you will remain focused in the present, and, in turn, the more you will be able to help others to do the same.

More, Please?

▶ A woman was eating at an expensive restaurant. She ordered a pricey meal that she absolutely despised. When the waiter asked her how it was, she replied, "I hate it. It's terrible, and it's too expensive for me!" Then she paused and asked, "May I have some more, please?"

"What?" asked the waiter, dumbfounded. "If you don't like it and it's too expensive, then why would you order more?"

The woman was speechless. She didn't know why. But she insisted on having more, nonetheless. ◀

The woman in the story might seem foolish for ordering and paying a lot for something she despised, but how often are you and I like her? How many of your own precious, limited thoughts, for instance, do you allow to be consumed by things that you despise and are far too costly for your mental, physical, and spiritual well-being? Although you can order whatever you want from the eternal menu of universal content to fill your inner thoughts, how much time do you spend ordering and devouring the things that anger you? Unlike the woman in this story, it's wise for you to order only the kind of information that you actually want to have in your mind, because whatever you fill your mind with will be in your mind, and you are paying for it one way or another.

The Story of the $450

▶ A man who had recently been released from prison was talking to a teacher. This man was visibly enraged as he told the teacher that his wallet with $450 in it had just been stolen, he had a strong suspicion who had stolen it, and he was going to seek out the man, get his money back, and kill him.

The teacher asked the former prisoner how long he'd been incarcerated. "I was down for eight years, and I just got out," the man replied.

The teacher then asked, "Did you like your time in prison?"

"What?" The man stared at the teacher. "Did you ever spend time in prison?"

"No."

"I didn't think so," said the man angrily.

The teacher prodded further. "In all that time in prison, were there ever moments when you wanted to get out?"

The former inmate seemed to get even angrier. "What's wrong with you? Of course I wanted to get out!"

Unfazed by his anger, the teacher asked, "How badly did you want to get out?"

The man, now visibly more agitated, stared down the teacher. "I wanted to get out every second of every day!"

"What would you have done to get out?"

"I would have done anything!" said the former inmate, stepping aggressively toward the teacher.

The teacher looked piercingly back into the eyes of the angry man and finally asked, "Would you have paid $450?"

The man stopped. The teacher's words moved through him. He realized that if he killed the man who stole his $450, he would end up back in prison (probably for life). His anger left him. He thanked the teacher and walked away. ◀

Now, this is a true story. I was the teacher, and the man was in one of my anger management groups. Now that you know this a true story, you probably want to know the rest of what happened. The man was calm enough after talking to me that he went home and slept instead of seeking out the man he believed to be the thief. In the morning, when he awoke, he said a thankful prayer that he didn't go after that man and end up in prison again. In fact, he even imagined that he paid the amount that was stolen from him and was now free. He felt so good knowing that he resisted acting on impulse that he decided to clean his room. As he was picking a pile of clothes off the floor, he found his wallet with the $450 in it.

This man's contact with a creative solution to sparking insight in him changed the course of his life. Moreover, because he was able to genuinely gain from the lesson, he shared his experience with our group the following week, which had a profound impact on several other people, including me. So the benefits rippled outward, like a pebble in a pond.

All the actions we take today will affect us one way or another in the future. Sometimes, when we make a mistake, we would be willing to pay any price to take it back—all the more reason why it's advisable to think through what we're going to do ahead of time. The pressing question to ask yourself from this story is: How much would you pay to avoid making the mistakes of the future? First and foremost, reflect on how much you might actually pay to avoid mistakes that you could potentially make from a place of impulse. Next, work as hard as you can on your self-talk and self-discipline so that you can avoid making such mistakes.

You already know that you master what you practice. Once you have figured out how much you'd pay to gain the self-control that will bring you the future results you want, you can use the currency of your time and effort to get it. Finally, from a place of clarity and experience, do your best to share the insight that you gain from this conscious perspective of the inevitable future with those who need it most.

Why Creativity Matters

Our emotions really are designed to teach us something. Consider our prelinguistic ancestors. Love would have taught bonding, which ultimately led to group mentality and helped the survival of the species. Fear meant one should be alert to danger, and, again, that meant survival. Sadness meant that group members mattered, and we are more likely to look out for and protect that which matters to us, which is pretty useful in the grand picture of the longevity of a species. Anger might have motivated our early ancestors to protect their resources (for example, if you steal my resources, I get angry and fight to protect them, thus having resources to survive), find motivation to avoid pain (the angrier you are, the more you lash out, and the more you lash out, the more endorphins are released), or heighten desire to track down the bigger prey that could subsequently feed more of the group (anger itself is not wrong or bad and, in fact, can be a very strong motivator), which in turn helped the individual survive. Each of our basic emotions conceivably served an evolutionary purpose before language evolved. Once language evolved, creativity blossomed. With creativity came ineffable beauty, as well as intolerable self-inflicted pain.

It's helpful to be mindful both of the ways in which creativity exacerbates problems and the ways in which you can bank on creativity to learn from your emotions and teach others to learn from theirs. Teaching stories and metaphors are layered so deeply that the extent of their impact can be truly understood only on a case-by-case basis and over time. Ultimately, each person feels the depth and reach of metaphors and teaching tales on an indescribable level. The more you can tap into creativity to spark awareness, the more you can in turn help others tap into their own.

Whether you hone in on your awareness of the ways in which your self-talk drives your narrative and, subsequently, your emotions, or whether you focus more on the ways in which you can use experiential awareness or teaching tales to spark insight in others, the reality is that there is tremendous power in creativity. Ultimately, you or anyone else in a creative state is not in a state of conflict. Creativity brings depth to your experience of life, and it helps you walk straight through any anger or conflict head on.

Finally, people learn in different ways. Some techniques you try will work well with some people and not at all with others. Through the lens of Yield Theory, everyone's perspective matters, so do your best to assess the most effective way to get through to the person who is in front of you. When you draw on analogies and metaphors, including experiential and visual techniques, you are more likely to meet diverse learners where they are. At all times, keep in your foreground the goal at hand: to use your creativity to find ways to spark insight, both in yourself and in those on whom you hope to have an impact.

Summary

Creativity is one of the greatest strengths we possess as humans. Unchecked, however, creativity can manifest in negative ways and be an awful source of pain. It's important to learn the difference between consciously using creativity to help you solve problems and blindly allowing creative thinking patterns to spiral you or others downward. Insight helps us figure out our thinking patterns, and it can help us shift the way we see what we experience. Yield Theory utilizes creativity as a fundamental component most importantly because people have different learning styles. To help others walk through anger, it's not enough to simply have information, it's also vital to be able to convey that information to them in ways that actually work. The more you tap into your own creativity, the more options you have for communicating effectively with others, regardless of their emotional state.

He who gives way to violent gestures
will increase his rage.
CHARLES DARWIN

Mindfulness

Being in the Conflict

The world has many gurus but few masters. Gurus know their subjects; masters know themselves. The Buddha taught long ago that mindfulness is the path to immortality. In today's world, admittedly, "mindfulness" is a buzzword. It's far easier to throw the word "mindfulness" around in conversation than it is to actually implement it; and that seems even more true in times of conflict.

To be mindful is to be aware. That's it. The challenge for you is to be aware at all times of your thoughts, feelings, actions, and speech, as well as your presence, your environment, and what others are attempting to communicate to you, even under the duress of every intense emotion you experience. The idea of being aware of so much all at once can certainly seem overwhelming; nonetheless, mindfulness is vital to walking through anger in a conscious way. In this chapter, I'll show you why mindfulness is a fundamental component of Yield Theory and what it takes to be mindful as you listen, validate, and explore options with others.

▶ A professor approached the Zen master and condescendingly asked him what made him a "master of Zen." The master said, "When I eat, I eat. When I walk, I walk. When I talk to someone, I talk to that person." The haughty professor, who could barely keep himself from interrupting the master, replied, "That's ridiculous! Everyone does those things! And I guess since I do them, that makes me a Zen master, too." The master smiled and said, "To the contrary, when you eat, you think of other things. When you walk, your mind is elsewhere. And when you talk to others, your mind is not on what they're saying, but on what you'll say next. You are anywhere but present. That is the difference." ◀

To be aware of the present moment and what you're doing in such a complete way can take tremendous effort . . . until it doesn't. That is, being mindful takes practice until it just becomes the way you approach life. On the surface, presence might seem more achievable during routine tasks (like eating or walking or having a normal conversation) than in the midst of high conflict, but that's only if you equate being present with being calm. Being mindful of how you feel in the midst of intense or uncomfortable situations means, not trying to control how you feel, but tuning in to how you *do* feel. Ultimately, mindfulness is about becoming the objective observer of yourself.

The more you get to know yourself, including understanding the root of your thoughts and the path they tend to take, the easier it will be for you to identify what triggers what in you. With your heightened self-awareness, you will likely find being present becomes second nature. Presence is a way of being, and the key to presence is mindfulness, and the key to being effective at mindfulness is practice. That can start right now. For example, in this moment you may feel overwhelmed at the thought that the next time you have conflict, you're "supposed" to be aware simultaneously of all your thoughts, language, how others are perceiving you, and what they're saying and doing, as well as figuring out how you're "supposed" to juggle all that *and* circumvent their fight-or-flight response. Practicing mindfulness in this moment, right here and now, simply means being aware of those racing thoughts and how they make you feel. In reality, in this exact moment, if you are paying attention to this sentence right now and nothing else, you are practicing mindfulness.

Humans have always had to deal with distractions, but perhaps never more so than in our current milieu of social media, 24/7 news cycles, and instant mobile connectedness. Just observe people in public places as they walk alongside friends or sit in coffee shops while they use their phones to text or talk to someone else. Distraction is now the normal context of our communication. That means that almost any attempt you make to reach the minds and emotional centers of others is like walking through a forest that has no neatly paved path; the trees—the many distractions—get in the way. Most of us live in such forests. You need to create a path through your own "forest of distraction" before you have any chance of reaching someone else who is also living with distractions. Mindfulness is that path.

To master communication is to accurately understand how others are receiving what you're saying, so that from moment to moment you can make the adjustments necessary to ensure the message you intend to convey is actually heard. The question we are constantly asking ourselves in Yield Theory is: How can I meet ever-shifting others where they are? To answer that is to be mindful of your thoughts, feelings, speech, tone, body language, energy, and presence. It's about understanding the role you play in every interaction, as well as making ongoing informed assessments of the ways in which what you say and do affects others. Mindfulness is, like the core of Yield Theory, simple to understand but often difficult to practice. Most people probably perceive themselves to be more mindful than they actually are.

▶ Four Zen students were told to sit in complete silence. The first said out loud, "I know I can sit in silence, no problem." The second said, "You just spoke!" The third said, "You both are fools!" And the fourth said, "I am the only one who has not spoken." ◀

Like these Zen students, how many of us are quick to judge others but slow to be aware of ourselves? Recognizing that we are self-aware creatures is one of the characteristics that philosophers have used to distinguish humans from other mammals, but simply having the potential to be self-aware doesn't necessarily mean we always are. One of the biggest barriers to mindfulness is the ego. When your ego blurts out, "I already do that," it's likely relying on hindsight bias to convince you that you "already know about mindfulness," which puts up an obstacle to your actually practicing it. The "I already do that" mind-set places the onus for more effective communication on others, rather than you continuously coming back to you focusing on controlling yourself. Think back to the story of the Great Watermelon Slayer, who didn't blame the people of that stale futuristic world for what they believed. Instead of proclaiming he "already knew" what the water-melon was, he made the effort to meet them where they were and discover the watermelon with them.

Be mindful that your ego will attempt to convince you that you're "right" or that you "already communicate effectively." Awareness of the ego's tricks will make it easier for you to meet others where they are. The more demanding you are that others come to you, the more you operate out of the Critical Parent ego state, and the more you will lead with arrogance rather than humility. Remember, arrogance is like gasoline on a fire in any conflict. If you keep in your foreground just how much there is to be mindful about in every given moment, you will naturally lead with humility.

Mindfulness is not an academic concept or one that can ever be completed: It's an ongoing way of life that is relevant in every waking moment. But what a challenge to be constantly mindful! After all, how much of our lives do we drift through in an unaware state? Think about how many present moments you might have missed because you were thinking about the past, worrying about the future, or living in some cartoon world of your own creation. The past is gone, and it's not physically possible to live in the future, so the only moment that actually exists is the present. With your brain's default-mode network sending between 50,000 and 70,000 thoughts through your mind every day, it doesn't seem possible to keep track of all of your thoughts all of the time. What you can real-istically keep track of, however, is what thoughts are going through your mind *right now*. The more present you are in each moment, the easier it is to be mindful, and vice versa.

Be Mindful of Your Thoughts

Thoughts are arguably the fuel of the greatest power that we as humans wield. It was our capacity for higher-level creative thinking, after all, that helped us separate ourselves from all the other species on our planet, even though many other creatures are incredibly more physically adept than we are. And on a strictly individual level, your thoughts are so powerful that they actually have an impact on and ultimately define your experience of life. Life is what it is. What you tell yourself, however, influences whether you experience, for instance, the struggles you encounter as challenges to overcome in the adventure story of your life, as impassible barriers, or maybe even as psychological jailers that imprison you and stop you from moving forward. Your thoughts shape the larger picture of meaning (or lack thereof) that you create or discover in your life, as well as the context and actuality of your everyday interactions. To be mindful of the way your thoughts drive your experiences is the key to being able to change or embrace them. Again, as the Buddha taught, "As you think, so you become."

If you're not mindful of the way your thoughts influence your experience, you can be bounced from one state of mind to the next like a steel ball in a pinball machine. In chapter 7 I discussed how extreme language creates extreme emotions. Now, let's take a look at how mindfulness can be applied to steer away from that. The following extreme-language-based thoughts—the kinds of statements our cartoon-world perspective comes up with—can radically and unnecessarily increase your anger. These lines of internal dialogue reflect both what people might say to themselves, as well as outright say or share with others:

1. "You never listen to me!"

2. "You always do . . . !"

3. "I guess you're saying no one should ever be . . ."

4. "Everyone is against doing . . ."

5. "You can't say that!"

6. "He shouldn't have done . . . !"

7. "She shouldn't have been there!"

8. "No one ever does anything around here!"

9. "I can't stand it when people do . . . !"

If you're not mindful that extreme language—including the language of your self-talk—produces extreme emotions, then you might allow yourself to be batted around by whatever occurs in the outside world, forever giving your control away to anyone or anything that doesn't fall in line with your cartoon-world view. By making the simple shift to being mindful of what you think and of the impact those thoughts have on your reality, you empower yourself to control your perception of anything you experience, and you can balance the wording accurately when you state your thoughts to others. Although the shift is simple to understand (that is, your thoughts affect your experience), it takes practice to master. The first step in changing your thoughts is to be mindful which thoughts you have. The more mindful you are of your thoughts, the more authentic you can be to your core, and the more you practice being aware of your thoughts, the better you will get at telling yourself the types of things that can help you handle life in the most effective way possible.

When it comes to experiencing anger or handling conflict, the thoughts you choose to use to describe what is happening will directly affect how severe that experience will be. It might not feel like you're relying on extreme language to describe your inner experience of something, but one way to gain insight on whether you are is to observe the strength and/or intensity of your reactions. Obviously, the stronger the reaction you're having, the more intense the self-talk you're engaging in. Of course, some situations are life-threatening and genuinely warrant extreme reactions. Gaining awareness of your self-talk doesn't negate your ability to respond intensely when you actually need to. It does, however, help you not to react unnecessarily strongly.

Balance begins with the words you use to describe your experiences to yourself and others. For instance, consider the nine examples I gave above of common cartoon-world thoughts. Here are some ways we might restate them in accurate language. This time, imagine saying these statements out loud to others:

1. "It doesn't seem like you listened to what I said earlier."

2. "I experienced you doing that on two different occasions." (Be specific instead of using the blanket, extreme descriptor "always.")

3. "If I hear you accurately, you're saying that you don't think I should . . ."

4. "I've talked to X number of people today who were against that idea." (Again, be specific rather than saying "everyone." Remember, too, that there are more than seven billion people on the planet, so for "everyone" to believe the same thing is not likely. Even if you want to refer to "everyone in the room," it's wise to clarify. For example, "Everyone in that particular group I talked to this afternoon seemed to be on board for this . . ." is more accurate and specific than the much vaster "everyone," which we typically use to feel validated in our perspective.)

5. "I'd rather you didn't say that" or "If you're going to say that, it's smart to be mindful of the outcome."

6. "I wish he hadn't done that, but it's not the end of the world."

7. "I wish she hadn't been there, but she was."

8. "I don't feel like I've gotten as much support as I'd like recently." (This more accurate statement is significantly less antagonistic than the unrealistic and quite impossible statement that "no one ever does anything around here.")

9. "I don't like it when people do . . . , but I can handle it." (The more you own responsibility for your likes and preferences while simultaneously realizing the reality that your "not liking" something is significantly less threatening than literally "not being able to stand" something, the less reactive you will be, and the less likely you'll be to elicit others' fight-or-flight response.)

Be Mindful of Your Feelings

Your physiological feelings come from more places than just your thoughts. It is possible, after all, to have completely peaceful thoughts but still feel physiologically agitated or irritable. We know that how you feel can be influenced by your thoughts, but your thoughts do not *determine* how you feel altogether. The reality is that multiple factors have an impact on your feelings. However your feelings arise, though, the fact is that they influence the way you communicate, so it's wise to be mindful of them.

It doesn't take deep self-reflection to recall times when you've snapped at others or responded more intensely than the situation warranted. You are human, after all, and it's perfectly natural to misread interactions or respond more emotionally than necessary. When you feel agitated or irritable, your emotional center is activated, and it can be challenging for you to exude patience. At a minimum, it's important to understand that physiological feelings of agitation or irritability can contribute to you experiencing a situation in a way that's a bit magnified. In short, mindfulness of how you feel can help you align your expectations with the reality that additional factors might be intensifying your experience.

Even when we're in our most Zen-like mental space, we might have slept only four hours, be in pain, or be taking medicine that alters our physiological feelings. From incalculable serotonin and dopamine deficiencies to pain receptors being flooded with high-alert messages, your body might physiologically feel off, even when your self-talk is balanced. Being mindful of your physiological feelings and communicating what you're feeling to others can take you a long way toward clarifying obstacles in communication.

Because it's important in Yield Theory to be true to the way you authentically speak, I'm reticent to give exact phrases for you to use, but here's an example of a way that I might share what I'm feeling with others: "I can tell that my body is feeling a little more anxious than I'd like right now, and I want to be mindful that this feeling is likely affecting the way I'm experiencing this moment." For me, letting others know what's going on with me does at least three things. One, it models mindfulness to others. Two, it helps me share an aspect of what I'm experiencing that's invisible but obviously playing a role in my interaction. And third, it depersonalizes the feeling so I can separate myself from it (in other words, it reminds me that I am not my feelings). I might literally phrase the feelings I have in the way I wrote them above; for you, it's important to use words that fit with the way you authentically communicate. Either way, the message is the same: Be genuine about saying what your body is physiologically feeling, because doing so can help you circumvent others' fight-or-flight response.

Throughout my career I have studied countless hours of videotaped counseling sessions. One of the patterns I've consistently noticed is that when counselors acknowledged the ways in which their feelings might be contributing to the interaction, it elicited a similar type of response from clients. It also seemed to deepen the connection between them, as evidenced by subsequent disclosures of new personal information. Therapeutic interactions aside, however, it just makes practical sense that how you feel contributes to the energy you bring to your interactions and that others can and do pick up on any incongruence between what you're feeling and what you're saying. What common sense says (and clinical observations confirm) is that it's more effective to acknowledge the elephant in the room than to ignore it.

Sharing what you're feeling doesn't mean that you then have to shift the focus of the conversation onto you. It is possible to simply acknowledge that your feelings are contributing to your experience of the present moment without going into further detail. For example, you could say something along the lines of, "I want to let you know that I can tell my body feels off right now, and that has nothing to do with you, but just in case it's affecting how I'm coming across, I wanted you to know." The more straightforward and honest your statement, the better.

Being mindful of your feelings and sharing the gist of them are important ways to clear away potential psychological obstacles that might be impeding clear communication. But in the actions of listening, validating, and exploring options, it's crucial to understand that briefly acknowledging your feelings is not intended to communicate that you, too, are suffering in some way. It's not about dipping into your Hurt Child ego state to elicit sympathy from others; it's entirely intended to exude mindfulness. In supervising hundreds of people in my career, the only time I've seen disclosing how you're feeling be unhelpful has been when the person is perceived as attempting to shift the focus of the conversation to themselves. When it comes to feelings, anger is not wrong or bad in and of itself; neither are sadness, happiness, fear, or any other feelings. Your ability to have feelings is an evolutionary trait hardwired into your being. Your gut feelings can guide you when they are, in fact, gut feelings, and not feelings shaped by self-talk. As I've told my clients for years, "Your gut feelings are designed to save you, but your self-talk-induced feelings are designed only to shake you." Mindfulness can help you understand that difference.

For example, it's wise to trust the physiological feeling of fear if that felt sense of danger steers you away from a threat to your safety. Fear that arises when you stand on the edge of an enormous cliff is rational and helpful, designed to protect you and keep you from randomly jumping. Listening to rational fear will keep you alive longer than, say, fearlessly jumping off the cliff would. On the other hand, a thought along the lines of "I'm afraid the wings on this airplane are going to fall off halfway through this flight" is indicative of fear that's more likely driven by irrational (if highly creative) self-talk. The challenge is to discern the difference between helpful fear and created fear. That's why it's essential to be in tune with your thoughts and feelings on a regular basis and to practice being mindful of the ways in which your thoughts influence your emotions, as well as the way your emotions influence your communication.

Be Mindful of Your Physiological State

Since a core teaching in Yield Theory is that your mind always wants to match your body, it's vital to be mindful of what's going on in your body, as well as what story your mind might be creating to make sense of your physiological state. The more you can recognize what's happening in your body, the more easily you will be able to decipher why your mind is creating the story it is. In contrast to just being mindful of your physiological emotions, it's equally important to also be mindful of your entire physiology. For example, the feeling of nausea is uncomfortable and can significantly impact your energy, yet it is not an emotion. There are more common physiological impacts as well, and understanding some basic physiology can be a great help toward that end.

The brain region that perhaps plays the most central role in what I would call unnecessary anger and conflict is the *hypothalamus*. The hypothalamus is seated deep in the limbic system of the brain and is responsible for handling a few important functions that, if left unchecked, can impact conflict-related communication in a big way: (1) hunger and thirst, (2) fatigue, and (3) body temperature. A "hypothalamus triple punch" is what I call the phenomenon of being hungry, tired, and overly hot all at once. But even if experienced one at a time, hunger, fatigue, and rising body temperature can add to agitation, irritability, and, ultimately, anger.

"Hangry" is the portmanteau of the words "hungry" and "angry," and we owe thanks to the hypothalamus for bringing this word into the lexicon of the English language. When you're hungry, you feel agitated and irritable, and that of course leads to a short temper and lashing out or snapping at others. A recent study by Jennifer MacCormack and Kristen Lindquist showed that being hungry isn't quite enough to contribute to hanger, as the added element of confusion or uncertainty also significantly contributes to it.

So if you're hungry, unsure, and agitated, you have the complete recipe for hanger. You don't need scientific studies or psychological jargon to make you aware of how hanger has impacted your own life. Think of any unnecessary arguments you've had with loved ones that were caused by one or both of you being hungry. Think, too, of the trouble you might have saved yourself had you learned long ago to be mindful of the impact hunger has on your mood, especially coupled with the information that your mind always wants to match your body. When your body felt agitated from hunger, your mind made up a story (usually about the shortcomings of your loved ones) to make sense out of that feeling. Most adults can recognize this kind of hunger-driven behavior in toddlers but fail to see it in other adults or in themselves.

Fatigue has a similar impact on the hypothalamus. The old adage "Never go to bed angry" probably was well-intentioned advice for dealing directly with what needs to be dealt with; however, taking this advice literally can spark unnecessary anger and conflict. Just as it responds to hunger, the hypothalamus goes on alert under the influence of fatigue. The result is heightened emotion that contributes to, rather than lessens, conflict. As I have taught clients in anger management for years, "By all means, go to bed angry, and if you wake up still mad, keep fighting then. But if the only reason you're fighting is that one or both of you is tired, then you will be grateful that you got some sleep." Yield Theory requires us to be mindful of our physical energy or our lack of it, just as we should be aware of hunger.

Body temperature, too, can increase agitation and irritability, likewise resulting in avoidable conflict. When you're overly hot, especially, you can feel so agitated that your mind makes up a story associating your uncomfortable physiological state with those around you. Recognizing that you are experiencing physiological discomfort can radically shift the course of your communication. You can say something along the lines of, "I'm really sorry, but I can feel myself being agitated, and I recognize that my agitation is likely rooted in how uncomfortably hot I am right now." Or: "I can feel how tired I am, and I'm aware that when I'm this tired, I'm making more out of things than I might if I were rested; so I'm open to keep talking, but I think it might be more effective if I could get some sleep right now." Or even something shorter, like, "I'm really hungry, and I can tell I'm superagitated right now." The exact wording in the way I phrase these statements might or might not resonate with you, but the point is to notice what's happening in you and then own the impact it's likely having.

When you recognize hunger or thirst, fatigue, and body temperature as sources of agitation, as well as acknowledge the reality that your mind wants to match your body, you will avoid unconsciously adding to conflict or free yourself from unneeded conflict altogether. Bringing your internal discomfort into your foreground allows you to make it a part of an open dialogue; essentially, it affords you the opportunity to be accurate about that particular component of the conflict. Once you notice what's happening inside you, you can set it aside. It's as if you are going through a box filled with different items, each representing a part of the conflict: Acknowledging whatever's affecting your hypothalamus is akin to removing one item in that box.

Be Mindful of Your Tone

"I love you!" she screamed angrily as he threw the chair violently across the room.

"I love you!" she exclaimed with joy.

"I love you!" she said with platonic laughter.

"I love you!" she said sarcastically.

"I love you!" she said, crying.

"I love you!" she whispered excitedly.

When it comes to *what* is said and *how* it's said, the same words can mean things as different as night and day. Throughout this book, I have brought up the difference between content (the words you say) and process (how you say them). Being mindful of your tone allows you to consciously communicate in a manner that is congruent with how you feel *and* with the message you hope to convey. Although it would be great (in my cartoon world) if children learned the significance of tone of voice when they originally learn language, usually the first time children are made aware of it occurs with a curt warning: "Watch your tone!" The irony is that the advice to "watch your tone" can actually be helpful *if* it's said in the right tone.

Anecdotally, it's difficult for me to say just how many couples I've watched argue through the years over the tone of their communication. "I did say that!" is the response many people give when their partner indicates what they didn't say. Think of your own experiences.

How many miscommunications have occurred in your relationships due to tone?

When you're walking through anger and handling conflict head on, being mindful of your tone is crucial. When the Buddha taught that anger will never be overcome by anger, my sense is he understood that if your tone is interpreted as threatening, then others will continue to respond in kind. If, however, you can be mindful of controlling your tone and, furthermore, lead with peace, you'll have a significantly better chance to remain in control of your own feelings through the interaction.

Recall transactional analysis from chapter 7. Your tone often sets the stage for how others interpret your ego state. You do not have to yell or be physically intimidating, for instance, to be demanding in your tone (Critical Parent). A subtle shift in the way you say something can mean the difference between communicating from your Parent or Child ego state to communicating from your Adult. Remember also that you see your intentions, but others see only your actions, so regardless of what you mean, others are only experiencing what you're showing them. In speaking, your tone of voice is often more telling than the actual words you use.

Since you can't see or experience your tone from others' perspectives, mindfulness is key. By observing how others respond to what you say, you can get a more accurate sense of how they might be experiencing your tone than by simply relying on your own assessment—especially since any assessment we make of our own communication tends to include our intentions.

Be Mindful of Your Physical Presence

If there was a way to accurately measure what causes the largest gaps between what you see in your interactions and what others see, I believe that physical presence would make the top of the list. From your size and what you look like to your posture and the physical position you're in to the way you move in relation to those with whom you're communicating, your physical presence influences conflict more than you likely realize. You see others, whereas others see you—so being mindful of your physical presence to the extent that you can is very important. I cannot stress enough that, regardless of your intentions, people see only what is presented to them on the outside, so an accurate self-assessment of your interactions is best based on what others actually see.

To begin with, your physical presence is what it is: From how tall you are to how much you weigh, your physical size is what your physical size is. There are only a limited number of ways that we can impact our physical presence. The good news is that there are no body types or physical characteristics that hold a monopoly over handling conflict more effectively than any other body types or physical characteristics. We can, however, become more aware of how others are perceiving us. In other words, to be a great communicator or to handle conflict well, it doesn't matter what you look like in any way, shape, or form; it only matters that you're *aware* of what you look like, because, like it or not, your physical presence plays a role in every in-person interaction that you have.

Because we know our intentions, it makes sense that we might minimize or downplay the role our physical presence plays in conflict, but logical or not, other people still only see what they see. For example, I'm six feet tall, weigh 250 pounds of mostly muscle and a Buddha belly. I have a shaved head, a beard, and visible tattoos. I usually dress in jeans and a T-shirt, so I take it lightheartedly when people ask me, fairly frequently, if I'm aware that I look like I just stepped out of a biker bar. My presence can be viewed as intimidating by some people, so I'm mindful to account for that when I'm interacting with others. One time I was speaking at a maximum-security female state prison. Afterward, an inmate came up to me for an autograph. She looked up at me with her much smaller frame and said, "You're scary." Although I could obviously see that I towered over her, I couldn't help but be aware that she was convicted of killing another woman over not being paid for drugs, so the fleeting, lighthearted thought "My life is centered on bringing people peace, and you killed someone for not paying you, and you think I'm scary?" came to mind. But I was also aware that to her, I *was* scary looking. Our perception is reality.

One of the most powerful concepts from the world of counseling that directly translates to everyday communication is *transference*.

Transference is the perception people have of others in their lives that they transfer onto you. In other words, you might remind one person of a beloved relative and remind another person of a childhood bully. You have no say over the transference others put onto you, especially as you initially interact with them. The more mindful you are of your physical presence, the quicker you will be able to assess if others are reacting to what you're currently exuding or what you might remind them of from their past. The goal in walking through anger directly is to connect with others, and the heart of Yield Theory is circumventing others' defensiveness, so it's wise to spend more time assessing how others perceive you (in the real world) than focusing on how you think they "should" perceive you (from your cartoon world).

In all, the more you assume the posture of a kind, confident, compassionate, and nonthreatening person, the more your mind will likely follow suit, and, ultimately, you will have a better chance of being interpreted that way by others. Remember also that other people's mirror neurons are evaluating the way you present physically and that threatening gestures are assessed as dangerous, even if you don't mean for them to be. The more you can assume the posture of a peaceful being, the more likely you will elicit a similar reaction in others. At a minimum, however, the more peaceful your posture and movements, the safer others perceive you to be, and the less defensive they have to feel, which gives you a better chance to open the doorway to being able to communicate more clearly.

Let Me Sit Down for a Minute

In a conflict situation, when you are practicing mindfulness of your physical presence, one of the most practical strategies you can use is to sit down whenever possible. Standing overtop of someone is an intimidating position for anyone, but especially so in times of conflict, and even more so if a larger person stands overtop of a smaller one. I teach men, for instance, that standing overtop of their wives or girlfriends in an argument or disagreement can be intimidating and elicit the fight-or-flight response, even if they never have and never would hit that person. At the biological level, it comes down to being aware that males are generally physically larger and stronger than females. This is significant to bring to the foreground, because denying this reality only augments the cartoon-world perspective and contributes to unintended (but very clear) intimidation. Once you're aware of this, you can follow my very simple and straightforward advice: In any disagreement or argument, choose to sit down when it's possible.

Two things happen when you sit down. The first is that you take away the temptation to posture over others and, whether consciously or unconsciously, physically threaten them with your presence. Of course it's entirely possible that even sitting down you still might be intimidating, but at least you will lessen the perceived threat of your physicality, as opposed to using your body as a way of "sending a message." The second is that by sitting, you minimize the temptation to pace back and forth. Pacing increases testosterone, and excess testosterone leads to impulsivity—so pacing in anger essentially amps you up to explode. If the goal in handling conflict is to work through it and learn from it, then unconsciously adding proverbial gasoline to the fire is not wise.

Pacing back and forth also affects how you breathe, and how you breathe is related to how you feel. Essential to handling conflict effectively is the awareness that your presence is profoundly affected by the way you breathe. The anxious breathe rapidly, the angry breathe heavily, and the peaceful breathe calmly. In addition, the way you breathe signals your process to others. Sighing, for instance, is more likely to add to conflict than lessen it, because a sigh tends to represent exhaustion with the current conversation. Just as you can see when others sigh, others notice when you sigh, and they interpret your sighs in the same way you interpret theirs: as depletion. Sighing in conflict tends to imply that the other person simply cannot understand what you're communicating, and this is often interpreted as a shortcoming on their part, not yours. We often sigh when we don't feel understood, so the message others get is: "You still don't get it," which exacerbates conflict.

My rule of avoiding standing overtop of others in conflict especially applies to all parents, male or female, big or small. To state the humorously obvious fact, young children are smaller than their parents.

Without taking the time to get down on a knee and meet children at their eye level, parents constantly put children in a position of looking up at someone much larger than they are. In family anger and conflict situations, parents can radically shift the dynamics of the interaction by sitting down and emphasizing what lessons can be learned, rather than impulsively expressing their own emotions or, worse, standing overtop of their children. To stand overtop of a child and yell and then expect that child to "get" your lesson is as foolish as an intimidating giant standing angrily in front of you and trying to teach you a lesson. The odds are you will be so taken aback by the physical presence of the giant, you won't really hear what he's saying to you.

As you have seen, with Yield Theory, the idea is to imagine your interactions from the perspective of others. Nowhere is that more obvious than with how others experience your presence, despite this being a factor that is typically not in your foreground. Since your presence is inescapable, in physical interactions it's wise to be mindful of the ways in which others potentially perceive you. The more awareness you have of the ways others might experience your interactions, the better chance you have to adjust accordingly.

Be Mindful of Your Eye Contact

When you sustain eye contact with someone who is threatening, your testosterone level rises. As testosterone rises, so, too, do cortisol and adrenaline, all three of which prepare people to defend themselves (whether necessarily or unnecessarily). Knowing this and being aware that the mind wants to match the body will help you avoid sustained eye contact in conflict, both to prevent your own testosterone level from momentarily increasing and, perhaps more importantly, to avoid triggering excess testosterone levels in others. When others aren't aware that their mind wants to match their body, eliciting excess cortisol, adrenaline, or testosterone is rarely a good idea.

Eye rolling is dismissive and can trigger anger. The underlying message in eye rolling is something to the effect of: "What you're saying is so absurd and stupid that it's not even worth it for me to verbally respond, so I'm just going to roll my eyes." Dismissing someone's thoughts or emotions is equivalent to placing yourself above them, and from that space of hierarchy, it's difficult to validate from the core fundamental assumption of Yield Theory that we're all equal. Dismissing others is akin to being on a mountaintop hollering down at them. Although you might not mean to come across as thinking, "I believe I'm better than you," eye rolling essentially conveys that message.

Another important fact to understand is this: Those with limited assertiveness often shy away from making eye contact. It's easier, after all, to look away from someone and declare a strong opinion than it is to look at someone directly and communicate something that might be perceived as controversial. Once I was addressing a group of corrections officers who worked primarily in restricted housing units ("the hole"). I was talking about increasing understanding for inmates who have gone through significant trauma, and a corrections officer in the audience said—while looking away from me—"I don't care what happened to some people; some people are just scum and I'll always believe that. They're cowards, and that's a fact." He seemed to thrive in subsequent statements as long as he was able to avoid direct eye contact. I had a chance to talk to him during a break, however, and his demeanor changed significantly when I pointed out how lack of eye contact tends to embolden people to say whatever they want. Of course, I used Yield Theory to meet him where he was, so I listened to his concerns, validated how he felt, and then drew on an example in line with his own experiences of how, in his belief, the "scum inmates" communicate. My goal was to increase his awareness, so I thought of a situation that might resonate with him.

I told him, "I know it's so frustrating when inmates won't look at you in the eyes and then just spout off whatever they want at you. I know you guys have to deal with that stuff all the time. It's like this one experience I heard about where, when the doors in a restricted housing unit all opened accidentally, not one inmate came out. All those guys who talked so tough about what they would do if the doors were ever opened showed that, in reality, they weren't prepared to do any of what they said. They all just stayed in their cells."

I paused as he nodded in agreement. Then I said, "It's like they can avoid eye contact with you, because they know on some level that if they look at you directly in the eyes, they have to be accountable for what they say." Once I said that, his eye contact with me increased tenfold. Although he was exuding the same behaviors he didn't like in others, recognizing this was beyond his awareness until I used an example that awakened him. By using an example of others enacting the very behaviors he was engaging in, I essentially gave him an out: to choose either to continue to avoid eye contact (with a now heightened awareness of what this meant) or to engage. He chose to engage.

Once he was willing to look me in the eyes, he significantly softened the statements he was so sure about moments earlier. He was able to acknowledge that it makes sense that children who have been victimized would likely act out, and once he acknowledged that, I quickly inserted that understanding behavior doesn't mean excusing it, and that of course there still needed to be consequences for actions. This was the same statement I made in the larger group, and when he was able to avoid eye contact, he allowed himself to convince himself that there was no other side to his position; but once he was internally motivated to look at me directly (since he didn't want to replicate what the inmates whom he perceived to be "less than" did by avoiding eye contact), his stance softened, and he became more willing to see another side of the proverbial box.

Although too much eye contact or threatening eye contact can elicit others' fight-or-flight response, no eye contact allows people to get lost in their cartoon world and avoid psychological connection with others. The balance is important to understand. Mindfulness of your own eye contact, others' level of eye contact, and the ways in which eye contact enhances or impedes communication, especially in times of conflict, is essential.

Be Mindful of Your Energetic Presence

You bring energy to every situation you encounter, and you leave energy behind as you go. People respond to your overall presence, just as you respond to the presence of others, and your presence brings out certain patterns in them, just as theirs brings out patterns in you. The question is whether you are aware of the energy you bring to and leave behind in interactions. As you've seen throughout this chapter, mindfulness can help you gain the awareness that allows you to be more in control of your energy. Everything you are, everything you think, and everything you feel in the current moment contributes to the energetic presence you bring to a situation. The way you move and speak, the way you stand and sit, your eye contact, your tone of voice, what you key in on in conversations, how seriously you take yourself, and an unlimited number of other factors all contribute to your presence.

You can build your ability to give off an air of peace and strong, kindhearted energy through the practices of self-reflection, mindfulness, meditation, and compassion, which will help you walk through the fire of anger unburned.

Mindfulness Meditation: The Training Ground

We live in an era when science backs the centuries-old practice of meditation. Today, it's commonly accepted that meditation contributes to a healthy lifestyle as much as good diet and regular exercise. Scores of books and neurological studies have touted the physiological changes that occur in the brains of regular meditators. Meditation makes observable changes that are extremely beneficial, such as quieting the default-mode network (those interconnected neurons that contribute to our constantly running internal dialogue), decreasing unnecessary impulsive reactions, and increasing gray matter in areas such as the hippocampus (the memory center) and the cingulate gyrus (which regulates emotions and pain). Meditation has a direct effect on stress levels, concentration, perspective, health, sleep, happiness, mindfulness, and a sense of peace.

Although for some people the word "meditation" might still call to mind the image of a shaved-headed monk sitting cross-legged on a mountainside, the reality is that you can meditate anywhere you like, with any belief system you have, and you can even keep the hairstyle you currently have as well. There are different ways to meditate—different approaches and different philosophies—but an excellent place to start is with *mindfulness meditation*. The ultimate goal of mindfulness meditation is not quieting your mind, but observing it. There are more and less effective ways to practice mindfulness meditation, so here are some guidelines to consider incorporating in your practice.

1. Find a relatively quiet space if you can. (But be aware that, although it's ideal to have a quiet space, you do not *need* a quiet space in order to meditate. I teach meditation to inmates in some of the loudest environments extant, and they learn quickly that mindfulness meditation is not about controlling your environment but about being aware of what goes on within you when you cannot control the outside environment.)

2. Sit comfortably, with your back straight if possible. (Sitting up activates the reticular formation, the brain region associated with attention. You do not want to be too relaxed, as meditation is a form of paying attention. Whereas relaxation is necessary and wonderful, it is not the same thing as meditation.)

3. Do your best to sit as still as possible. (I love the saying "A still body is a still mind." The more you practice sitting still, the more you will quiet your mind.)

4. If you are in a spot where you feel safe and comfortable doing so, try closing your eyes so you're not distracted by visual stimuli. (As you progress in your practice, you might find, as many have, that keeping your eyes ever so slightly open is a helpful landing place.)

5. Slow your breathing down to a controlled, comfortable rhythm. (Sometimes it's helpful as you're starting out to engage in a type of "box breathing," where you inhale for a count of four, hold the breath in for a count of four, exhale for a count of four, and then rest in the silence at the bottom of the breath for a count of four.

Again, as you progress, eventually counting will likely give way to a naturally controlled breathing cycle.)

6. Be the observer. (In mindfulness meditation especially, there is no goal of thinking certain thoughts, repeating mantras, or doing anything other than practicing being present. A helpful way to do that is by "watching" yourself, almost as an outside observer who has unrestricted access to your mind would.)

7. In each breath, attempt to be as present as possible by focusing on the here and now.

As with anything you dedicate yourself to practicing, the more you do it, the better you get at it. Just as you wouldn't exercise a handful of times and expect to suddenly be a world-class fitness star, if you do not practice meditation regularly, it's unwise to expect to reap the kinds of benefits you can get if you do. I teach people that it's more important to be consistent with meditation than it is to sit once in a while for long periods. I usually invite people new to meditation to start with two minutes a day, until the act itself becomes a habit, and then to sit longer. Five minutes of meditation a day is a great target to aim for, especially if you can maintain consistency with that as a daily part of your life. If you're able to ultimately sit for ten minutes a day and, again, consistently do it every day, you are likely to reap the most benefits of meditation.

Over the last twenty years I've seen a lot of people get really excited to sit longer, and they get to twenty minutes quite quickly, but then they cannot realistically sustain taking twenty minutes to sit every day, so they fall out of the habit altogether. That is why it is better, from my perspective, for you to take just two minutes a day and meditate consistently and daily than it is for you to sit longer every once in awhile. Practicing even a little bit of mindfulness meditation regularly will benefit your body, mind, and spirit, and it will help you significantly with personal growth and self-awareness.

Summary

Becoming the objective observer of your thoughts, feelings, vocal tone, degree of eye contact, posture, physiological state, and energetic presence can seem like a lot, especially if you're trying to be mindful of all those things in the heat of conflict; but the more you practice being present in the moment, the easier being mindful in this way will become for you. In Yield Theory, practicing mindfulness involves not only being aware of yourself but also helping others become mindful of themselves. Through meditation, you can train yourself to be mindful in every moment—most importantly, in this one.

We need to talk.

SAID BY EVERYONE WHO HANDLES CONFLICT INEFFECTIVELY

The Five Errors
of Communication

What Not to Do!

Yield Theory is rooted in a philosophy that emphasizes what to do more than what to avoid doing. As you have seen with the seven fundamental components, the goal is to be intentional in your behavior and in the way you interact with others. Although to this point I have focused largely on what you can do to walk directly through anger and conflict, in the lighthearted spirit of balance, I believe it can be helpful to also know what not to do. In this chapter, you will see what I view as flat out some of the most ineffective ways people handle conflict. In other words, you will learn exactly what not to do!

The Five Errors of Communication

I developed and refined the whole methodology of Yield Theory because I spent so much time observing people shut others down with what they said or the way they said it, even when the information they had to share was valuable and fitting for the person they were talking to. My work has led me to identifying five basic errors of communication that people commonly make: error of approach, error of interpretation, error of judgment, error of language, and error of omnipotence. In short, these are the five things not to do when handling conflict.

Error of Approach

Ever present in Yield Theory is the idea that circumventing others' fight-or-flight response is paramount. The *error of approach* describes what happens anytime you elicit others' fight-or-flight response from the moment you begin to interact. There are virtually unlimited ways we can do this, but some of the relatively common phrases I've noticed people use when making the error of approach are:

- "We need to talk."

- "Let me tell you why you're wrong/stupid . . ."

- "First of all . . ."

- "You need to calm down."

Let's take a look at each one.

"We need to talk" tends to immediately elicit defensiveness because—in American culture, at least—it is rarely followed by anything good. How often does anyone say, "We need to talk" and then go on to describe how perfect the other person is and how much admiration they have for the other person's flawlessness? Instead, "We need to talk" is all too often followed by a list of all the things the other person is doing "wrong" and "needs to change."

"Let me tell you why you're wrong/stupid . . ." is another way to instantly trigger other people's defensiveness, because stating this implies that you are not even considering exploring that person's ideas. Instead, this type of statement is the opposite of yielding to others.

"First of all . . ." is a phrase that suggests you are about to list all of the reasons why the other person is "wrong." This is a quick route to defensiveness because it signals you are about to go on a tirade against the other person rather than engage in a two-way conversation. Not only does giving a list of all the ways the other person is "wrong" shut the person down, but it also distracts them from even listening to you, because they are focused on what might come next.

"You need to calm down" is a phrase said from a place of fear. When you tell people that they "need to calm down" immediately, you are actually placing an unrealistic demand on them. People don't calm down because you tell them to; they calm down because you've given them the opportunity to express what was in their limbic system. They calm down because, as you've seen throughout this book, you've validated them enough to help "drain the limbic system," which allows them to move from their emotional center to their higher-level thinking center.

The other reason that demanding others calm down doesn't work is that—whether you want to be or not—you are telling them how to feel. Just as no one can tell you how to feel, you do not have the ability to tell others how to feel. Demanding that others feel differently from how they do is the exact opposite of Yield Theory. Remember that people see your actions, not your intentions, so regardless of whether or not it's your intention to put a barrier between other people and de-escalation, when you unrealistically demand that they feel any other way than they actually do, you are in fact adding to their obstacles rather than removing them.

The error of approach can be made in physical ways, too. Stepping too quickly or aggressively toward someone can naturally bring about defensiveness. Although that might seem wildly obvious to you, I have found that teaching this lesson in anger management groups is necessary, because almost every time I've introduced this concept, at least one group member has had trouble seeing it. People see their own intentions and are quick to make (often erroneous) assumptions about how others "should" be experiencing them. The fundamental component of mindfulness is in place to remind you to keep others' perspectives in the foreground as you interact.

Overall, the error of approach occurs anytime you shut others down from the moment you start to interact with them. Just as it's unwise to surprise a rhino, in conflict it's equally unwise to approach others in ways that elicit their defensiveness; rather, you want to prepare them to hear what you're about to communicate. To me, committing the error of approach is like putting yourself in a soundproof isolation tank with no windows and then wondering why others aren't hearing or responding to you. Although there's no foolproof way to ensure how others will receive what you say or how they'll experience your communication, there are certainly ways that will set you up for more success than others, as we've explored throughout this book. Committing the error of approach constitutes a definite "what not to do" in conflict.

To avoid committing the error of approach:

- Do not come at others without awareness of their natural defensiveness.

- Do not shut others down from the onset of communication.

Error of Interpretation

The *error of interpretation* occurs anytime you fail to accurately understand what others are communicating. The error of interpretation seems to be made most frequently in two ways: (1) by focusing too much on content over process and (2) by listening through the earpiece of confirmation bias.

Step one in avoiding the error of interpretation is to be mindful to focus on process, more so than on content. Remember, just like you, others do not always say what they mean and can get tripped up on wording. Their process, however, is not something that has anything to do with being right or wrong or accurate or not; their process is rooted in how they feel, and people are not wrong or bad for their feelings alone. Being mindful of process allows you to more effectively assess what others are attempting to communicate.

Step two in avoiding the error of interpretation centers on confirmation bias. As you saw in chapter 4, the more you look for what you want to see in others, the more you will see it. Without an awareness of your confirmation biases, you can create huge barriers between you and those with whom you're attempting to communicate. Being wrapped up in confirmation bias is like standing with your nose to one side of the box and expecting to understand what others on completely different sides of the box are trying to show you. Once you recognize your confirmation biases, however, you can work to set those biases aside and genuinely listen to what others are expressing—like stepping back from your side of the box to see what is on the other sides.

The most direct way to account for the error of interpretation is to reflect what you are hearing others say and then accept their answer as to whether or not you are accurate with what they wanted you to hear. This can be done by simply saying something to the effect of, "If I'm hearing you correctly, I think you're saying . . ." By saying, "If I'm hearing you correctly," you are both owning the onus of communication on your end and giving the other person an opportunity to clarify or offer a different way of expressing what they want you to hear if you're off.

Again, using soft language like "I *think* you're saying . . ." is rooted in nonattachment and humility. After all, "I *think* . . ." is so much different than saying, "You said . . . !" which is rooted in attachment and certainty. When it comes to handling anger and conflict, nonattachment and humility will help you significantly more than arrogance and certainty.

To avoid committing the error of interpretation:

- Do not get caught up in content
  without recognizing process.

- Do not get tripped up by what you think you
  will hear and miss what is actually said.

Error of Judgment

The *error of judgment* occurs when we judge others rather than assess them. To *judge* is to give a moral evaluation, especially of a person's character, whereas to *assess* is to comment on the behaviors that you observe. Let's say that someone cheats on his girlfriend. The moral response might be: "He's a jerk!" The assessment is: "He continues to be unfaithful in his relationship."

The "moral high ground" is an excellent analogy for the error of judgment. The moral high ground is similar to the example I gave in the introduction of standing on top of a mountain and yelling down to people at the bottom of the mountain. First, they can't hear you. Second, it's not their responsibility to magically be able to appear next to you just because you want to tell them something (which is cartoon-world thinking). Instead, according to Yield Theory, it's your responsibility to go meet them where they are.

The error of judgment leads to shame, which, as I discussed in chapter 7, only perpetuates ineffective behaviors. The potential for everything great and everything terrible rests inside all of us, and in judging others, we seem to forget (or, at a minimum, ignore) the fact that we are somewhere along the same continuum as those we judge. Any action that any human being has ever done, after all, is human nature. What others choose to say and do might not be what you envision yourself saying and doing from the perspective you have known your whole life, but it's not possible for you to say definitively what you would have done had you lived as others (which is essentially the fundamental assumption of Yield Theory).

▶ The hand laughed at the foot. "You're such a puppet! What a fool! Don't you know you're just an extremity? You walk wherever you're ordered to go! I would never do that!"

The foot replied, "Don't you just follow orders too?"

The hand scoffed. "No, I grab what I want!"

But the other body parts chimed in and made the hand aware that he played a similar role as the feet. Conceding that point but no other, the hand said, "Yes, but at least I don't spend my days dragging on the ground . . ." ◀

Judgment is not only unwise and unhealthy to effective communication, it's also as foolish as the hand mocking the foot for doing a different form of what it itself does. Shadow projections occur when we judge in others the very things we are afraid to see in ourselves. "Yes, but I would never do . . . ," you say (and it's possible you might not ever do . . .), but there are others who can look at your actions and say the same thing.

Whether you view yourself as entitled to judge others or not, the pragmatic reason to be mindful of your judgments is that others tend to shut down when you shame them, and the primary goal of Yield Theory is to circumvent others' defenses so that you can be heard. Committing the error of judgment is like running a race in the wrong direction and then wondering why you never got to the finish line. At a minimum, be mindful of your judgments; at your best, learn to set them aside in favor of constant assessment.

To avoid committing the error of judgment:

- Do not judge others.

- Do not minimize or downplay the harm you've caused.

Error of Language

The *error of language* is similar to the error of approach in that it deals with the words that you use, but it differs in that the error of approach applies only when you begin an interaction, whereas the error of language applies to using extreme language at any point to elicit defensiveness. Awareness of the error of language permeates many aspects of Yield Theory, from conscious education to mindfulness to nonattachment. In any interaction you have, the goal is to be aware of what words elicit what responses in others.

Some of the most common errors of language occur when you use extreme and inaccurate descriptors: "You always do that!" "You never listen to me!" "We cannot keep doing this!" "I can't stand it!" In each example, the extremes can be countered by reality. If there's only *one time* the person has avoided doing what you're accusing her of "always" doing, it's not true. Only *one case* of the person actually listening, and again, saying that "you never listen" is inaccurate. Anytime you have continued fighting after saying, "We cannot keep doing this!" anytime you have kept bearing it after saying, "I can't stand it!" your actual ability to keep fighting or to keep bearing the situation empirically demonstrates that you're giving an inaccurate description. As you will recall from the process of assessment in the fundamental component of acceptance, it's important to be accurate in describing what you see and experience, and extreme language is rarely accurate.

To avoid committing the error of language:

- Do not use extreme words.

- Do not exaggerate.

Error of Omnipotence

The final error of communication is what I call the *error of omnipotence*. The error of omnipotence occurs when we assume responsibility for someone else's actions. At the end of the day, we are all only responsible for ourselves. As you saw with the concept of differentiation in the previous chapter on nonattachment, the goal is to give people your best and then let go of the outcome. It's to operate in the world as an individual emotional entity and not tie your self-worth or well-being to how others receive (or reject) what you offer. The error of omnipotence occurs when we convince ourselves that we are responsible for others' actions, but it's an error because we never are.

The specific term "error of omnipotence" comes from counseling literature. In their book *Impact and Change*, Bill L. Kell and William J. Mueller noticed that novice counselors would often tie their self-efficacy to how their clients were progressing. If their clients were doing well, they saw themselves as worthy counselors; if their clients were not doing well, they saw themselves as inadequate. Imagine if you were a counselor and saw ten clients in a single day. If your self-efficacy was tied to how your clients were doing and some were thriving while others were struggling, you would likely burn out of the profession in a very short time. Being centered in the only person you can control, you, is the most effective way to avoid the error of omnipotence. What I have found throughout my career is that the error of omnipotence extends well beyond the field of counseling. I believe it directly applies to all of us when we tie ourselves emotionally to the progress and actions of others.

Avoiding the error of omnipotence does more than help you stay centered: It also allows you to state consequences in a compassionate but nonattached way. For example, imagine that you're a manager and you implemented Yield Theory to handle a conflict between two of your employees. Let's say that "Bill" was caught spreading gossip about "Sally," and Sally then accosted Bill in front of customers, causing a scene. You called them both into your office, and then you listened to them, validated what you heard, and even explored options effectively. In this hypothetical scenario, let's further imagine that after you articulated the consequences to Bill and Sally—that either of them repeating the behavior in question would lead to termination—they both were able to articulate back to you that they understood. In other words, you laid out the consequences, and both Bill and Sally demonstrated they were clear on those consequences. An hour later, however, you walked in on Bill spreading gossip about Sally again, so you followed through with the consequence of firing him.

If you were to commit the error of omnipotence, you would convince yourself that it was somehow *your* failure that Bill continued to gossip. But you are not all-powerful. You are not responsible for Bill's actions. Bill's continuing to gossip was not a reflection of the way you handled the conflict. Instead, it was on Bill to own complete responsibility for his actions. Your job, from a Yield Theory perspective, was to listen, validate, and explore options (which, in this hypothetical scenario, you did very well). In so doing, you guided Sally and Bill to understanding the consequences of repeating their actions, as evidenced by their articulating back to you that they understood them. There could have been many reasons why Bill did what he did after your interaction, but none involved you "making" him do it.

Assessing potential reasons for why Bill continued to gossip can help you avoid making the error of omnipotence. For example, it's possible that Bill continued to gossip because he was embarrassed or hurt by something that happened. Although the only behavioral evidence you have for this potential assessment might be Sally's confronting him in front of others, it's probably not a stretch to think that the two colleagues might have had other interactions that were emotionally charged. (For example, maybe he wanted to go out with her and she rejected him, or maybe they went out and it didn't go well, or maybe they went out, it went well, and he had a pattern of sabotaging relationships in his life due to hurt he experienced in the past.) It's also possible that there were no deep-seated reasons for Bill doing what he did; perhaps gossiping was simply an ingrained behavioral pattern for him. Taking a moment to make that assessment would help you understand that his actions after he left your office were not disrespectful or personal toward you, but were instead a reflection of him. And they certainly were not "caused" by you.

Your identity cannot be created or destroyed on the basis of how others act. When you allow yourself to be emotionally enmeshed with others, you convince yourself that what others choose is a reflection of you. Just because you can be convinced of that, however, doesn't make it so. There is probably no more important time to understand the error of omnipotence than when it comes to how you handle conflict. People alone are responsible for the choices they make. Following the great line from the movie *Spider-Man*, "With great power comes great responsibility," I believe that once you are armed with the information presented to you in this book, it's your responsibility to put forth effort to implement the concepts in the best way you can. But once you've effectively listened, validated, and explored options—and done the best you can with what you have to work with in any given moment—the next healthy action you can take is to let go.

To avoid the error of omnipotence:

- Do not assume you are responsible for what others do.

- Do not base your self-worth on what others say or do.

The Interplay of Errors

All of the errors of communication can be thought of as linking together in a complicated five-circle Venn diagram. It's easy to see how something like confirmation bias can inhibit interpretation, lead to judgment, initiate extreme language that either shuts others down from the onset (approach) or during the interaction (language), and it certainly can lead to unnecessarily owning responsibility for others' actions (omnipotence). The point of identifying the five errors of communication is not to trip you up about which behaviors fall under which category; it's to offer you insight into ways that the communication mistakes you make might elicit others' fight-or-flight response. Evaluating your side of interactions takes primacy in Yield Theory, because you are the only one you can control. Being mindful of the five errors can help guide you through seeing what you say or do that might shut others down rather than circumvent their fight-or-flight response. The more you practice identifying the errors in general, the better you get at recognizing the ways in which you might make them, and the more easily you can avoid doing so.

Fossil Fuel for Awareness

During a paleontological expedition in the Gobi Desert in 1971, archaeologists discovered two well-preserved dinosaurs that appeared to have died simultaneously in combat: a Velociraptor and a Protoceratops. The Velociraptor had its piercing claw dug into the Protoceratops, and the Protoceratops looked like it was taking a bite out of the Velociraptor's arm. During their heated exchange, a sand dune collapsed on top of them, perfectly preserving that awful moment.

When I do professional speaking, I often show the actual photograph of these two fossilized skeletons intertwined, and then I give a made-up background on the two creatures. I usually say, "Imagine that these two creatures were nice little dinosaurs with nice little dinosaur families." I invite the audience to consider the entirety of these dinosaurs' lives. "They probably led lives that consisted of a great deal more than this final moment, but all we will ever know of them is this final moment. Now, this is nature, and predators hunt, and prey either fights, flees, or hides. Ultimately, both of these dinosaurs were so much more than this terrible moment, and yet this is all we know of these two individuals." And then I usually ask groups: "What do you think the odds were, despite the complexity of either of these two creatures' lives, that this terrible moment would be preserved?" And groups tend to agree that the odds were pretty astronomical. It's in that moment when I make this point: "In 2018, more than 2.5 billion cell phone cameras captured more than 1 trillion photos. So what do you think the odds are of your worst behaviors being caught and preserved forever?" That perspective is usually startling for the audience. I offer you the same question.

Any moment can, in fact, be your last, and anything you do is certainly more likely now than ever before to be captured in images or sound or both. If fear of being caught or having your worst moment preserved forever is enough to help you make wise decisions for your future self, it's probably helpful to use this anecdote frequently as fossil fuel for your decision-making. Now, my hope (admittedly from my cartoon-world view) is that you have more noble reasons to be kind, lead with compassion, and work through your anger without hurting others than just avoiding being caught or getting in trouble, but in reality, if fear of having your worst moment preserved for all time is enough of a motivator to help you make the most effective decisions for yourself and others, then I'll take it. Being constantly aware of how you come across to others might seem like an overwhelming task, but by now you know that it will get easier with practice.

A Few Final "Don'ts"

Some words, phrases, and actions are significantly more likely to add to people's defensiveness and unnecessarily stoke the fires of conflict. These few final "don'ts" highlight a word, a phrase, and an action that I strongly recommend you avoid unless you're aiming to increase conflict, not lessen it.

- Don't ask, "Why?"

- Don't say, "You said . . ."

- Don't assume you know what others feel.

Don't Ask, "Why?"

If the cornerstone of Yield Theory is circumventing people's fight-or-flight responses so you can talk to them in ways that can actually be heard, then it's essential to understand the impact the words you use have on others. One of the first words I teach people to avoid is "why." Think about the first time you might have heard the word "why." It was likely when you were a child and in trouble: "Why did you do that?!" In studying volumes of counseling sessions throughout the years, I have noticed that "why" tends to elicit almost immediate defensiveness in others. By shifting your language even slightly, you can still get to the reason behind why others do what they do, just without leading with that triggering word. Instead, consider saying something along the lines of, "What made you . . . ?"

Using a phrase like "what made you" does two things to circumvent the fight-or-flight response. First, this type of phrasing gives others an out to take. It's as if you're implying that something outside of them caused them to do what they did. Whether or not they choose to take that out provides you with an accurate assessment of their preparedness to change. For example, if people reply with, "So-and-so made me do it," that would indicate they aren't ready to assume responsibility for their actions. You might make the same assessment if they blame it on external factors (for instance, "My body was hurting so I lashed out"). In either case, by providing an out, you can assess whether others take that out or instead assume responsibly for what they did.

Second, by using "what made you"–type phrasing, you join with others to discover the source of their action, rather than accosting them with a head-on question that assumes they had a conscious motive (which is likely to trigger their defensiveness). Small tweaks in language can pay huge dividends in communication, especially in conflict. Avoid using the word "why" whenever possible; at a minimum, be aware of the impact using it can have on others.

You'll notice that I did not say, "Never use 'why.'" Sometimes, asking the question "Why?" will bring out of others exactly what you want. As a creative therapist, I sometimes handed my clients a marionette and had them imagine themselves as the puppet. After I had them bounce the puppet around a bit, if they said that they didn't like the idea of being tossed around like a puppet, I would ask, "Why not?" The reason? My goal was to have them forcefully defend their position of not wanting to be the puppet. In instances when you know what a "Why?" question is likely to elicit in others, it might be exactly what you want to use. Again, the goal isn't to avoid ever saying, "Why?"; it's to understand what the word tends to bring out of others and use it only if it aligns with what you hope to elicit in them.

I intentionally use the question "Why?" (more specifically, "Why not?") when people tell me that they are considering doing something irrational or harmful. I might say something along the lines of, "You say you want to hit him in the face—so why not?" I'm completely sincere when I'm asking that, because I know the response they give will tell me where they are in their stage of change and willingness to actually follow through with their threat. Again, I'm assessing how defensive they are of their idea. If they are quick to say, "I cannot do something like that for real," that tells me one thing; but if they hesitate and aren't sure of why not, then I stay with the conversation until we have talked out the most effective decision for them (and everyone concerned).

The point is that using the word "why" often elicits defensiveness, and if you are unaware of the way you use it, you are likely to spark defensiveness in others. If you are aware of how to use it to assess where others are, however, it can be an effective tool.

Don't Say, "You Said . . ."

The words "You said . . ." might seem innocuous, but that phrase can very much heighten defensiveness unnecessarily. When you use the phrase "You said . . . ," you are opening up the door for someone to be defensive. Even if you get the majority of what the person said accurately, if you are off by even one article, that person will likely zero in on the inaccurate part and defend it. Then the conversation becomes more about defending content than about getting to the heart of process.

One of the most helpful things you can do is replace that phrase with "I thought I heard you say . . ." or "If I'm hearing you correctly,

I think you're saying . . ." Again, you might think, "Why put so much effort into communicating?" and that's a perfectly valid question to ask. My answer is that if your goal is to talk so that you can actually be heard, then it's worth your effort to speak in ways that support that goal. Regardless of our cartoon-world thoughts that we "shouldn't have to" put so much effort into the details, the real-world truth is that the phrase "You said . . ." tends to elicit easily avoidable defensiveness.

Once, I was supervising a counselor in training, and we were reviewing her counseling video in a group supervision session. At one point in her video, I heard her use the phrase "You said . . . ," so I paused the video. I said to her (and to the group), "I want to stop this here, because I know this group jokes a lot about me emphasizing saying, 'I thought I heard you say . . .' instead of 'You said . . .'" The counselor put her head down, and her face became bright red; she was laughing to herself. I asked her what that was about, but she just shook her head and motioned for me to continue. I said, "With a client like this"— the client was an adolescent male who up to this point in the session had appeared to be combative with the counselor at every turn—"you really want to be mindful of using the phrase 'You said . . . ,' because I could see a client like this getting defensive about it, even if you were off by just one little word."

As I was saying this, I kept looking at my student, who was still laughing and shaking her head. She said, "Just play it." When I hit "play," the very next thing we saw was the client cutting her off, saying, "I did not say that!" The group burst out laughing, and so did the counselor. "As soon as I said, 'You said . . . ,' I could hear your voice in my head saying, 'I thought I heard you say . . . ,'" she confessed. "Then as soon as my client snapped at me that he didn't say that, I thought, 'Maybe I should skip supervision this week.'" We all laughed.

For the record, I rewound the tape, and she actually was extraordinarily accurate with her reflection of what she heard back to the young man. She only got one word wrong, and that was the part he immediately latched onto. It's great to be lighthearted and open to learning. I'm still in contact with that counselor, and we still laugh about that supervision session, ten years later.

Don't Assume You Know What Others Feel

There is an enormous difference between saying, "I understand what you're saying" and "I understand how you feel." Understanding the words that others speak is, of course, possible—that's communication. Saying, "I understand how you feel," however, is a great way to stir up defensiveness. The same is true with saying something along the lines of, "I know exactly what you're going through." The reason? You don't. You cannot completely understand how someone else feels, nor do you know exactly what others are going through, and no one can completely understand your subjective emotions, either. You can identify with anger if someone expresses anger. You know your *own* experience of sadness and anxiety and every other emotion. But to assert that you understand how someone feels is to state that you can entirely know something that is unknowable. Although your ego might insist that it "knows" and "understands," your authentic core likely respects others' experience as uniquely their own, just as it recognizes that your experience of reality is yours alone. Remember, needing to understand others is significantly less important than your constant attempts to *try* to understand.

One way to circumvent the desire to proclaim that you understand is to shift your paradigm regarding understanding itself. That is, give yourself permission to view understanding in the way you view knowledge: as always partial. Just the way you would likely admit that you have more to learn in life, it's equally helpful to admit there is always more to understand. From this vantage point, you can avoid your ego's best attempts to convince you that you have more understanding than you actually have. As you've seen throughout this book, humble energy is much more helpful for handling anger than arrogance and certainty.

Summary

People see your actions, not your intentions. You judge others by their actions but judge yourself by your intentions. We have a tendency to minimize the pain we cause others but maximize the pain they cause us. When you live in your cartoon world, you demand that others live according to your internal, made-up rules (or the way you believe the world "should" be); however, when you align your expectations with reality, you are more prepared to face the world as it is.

There are specific things you can do to shut others down or add to conflict. The five errors of communication are: error of approach (shutting others down from the moment you interact with them); error of interpretation (not hearing what others are actually communicating); error of judgment (judging rather than assessing others); error of language (using extreme language that triggers defensiveness); and error of omnipotence (believing you're responsible for what others say and do). Being aware of the five errors and avoiding making them is how you circumvent other people's defensiveness.

Finally, it's important to be aware of your presence. Not understanding how your physical presence, vocal tone, volume, and delivery are being received is likely to continually trigger defensiveness. The more aware you can be of what you say, how you say it, and the way you are experienced by others, the better chance you have to avoid the types of mistakes that can significantly add to anger and conflict.

Epilogue

The only way you can walk through conflict is . . . to walk through it! Ignoring anger and conflict or wishing them away does not make it so. Walking through anger can be done in many ways, but the most effective one involves leading with compassion, meeting people where they are, doing your best to see the world from their perspective, and then working your hardest to circumvent their defenses and to speak in ways that can be heard. The more you operate from your essence rather than your ego, the less attached you'll be to needing things to go the way you think they "should" go, and the more open you'll be to genuinely listening and learning about others. Once you hear others accurately, you will have a significantly better chance to deliver conscious information to them in ways that actually work for what they're ready to hear. With that kind of approach, you'll find you're able to bypass others' defensiveness and help them feel safe enough to be open to what you have to say.

Yield Theory offers a practical and efficacious methodology for handling conflict. It's not complex to learn, but it takes effort to master. You are already en route to mastering whatever communication style you currently practice, but when you practice Yield Theory, you are actively practicing the kind of communication style that will help you get around others' defensiveness, no matter how extreme, and to speak in ways that are actually heard. The more you learn about typical behavioral patterns, including the common effects of internal and external dialogue, and the more you understand and honor each individual's unique experience of existence, the better chance you have to see both the forest and the trees. The more you learn about your ego—including how it's triggered and how you can set it aside to approach others with humility (rather than meeting anger with more anger)—the better able you will be to connect with others in tremendously powerful and transformative ways.

Acknowledgments

As Lord Alfred Tennyson had Ulysses say when he arrived back home after being gone for twenty years: "I am a part of all that I have met." I always believed that the way he had Ulysses deliver that line encompassed my experiences entirely, as well. That being said, I am also so particularly grateful to Dorothy Hearst, Kelly Lenkevich, and everyone at Sounds True for their support, kindness, and tremendous guidance on this book. I'm beyond grateful to my parents for instilling in me an insatiable passion for learning and storytelling that are the basis of all the work I do. I'm indebted to my manager, Jeff Schwartz, and his incredible team: Aly Fingleton and Alan Eisenson (who have believed in me and supported me for years), and to my incredibly hard-working literary agent, Jill Marr, for helping this project come to fruition. I most especially want to thank my daughter, Kaia, for being who she is and for inspiring me every single day (this book, as is everything I do, is for you, Kaia). Finally, I want to acknowledge and thank my wife, Kristen, who read every word of every version I wrote of this book, and who stood by me and listened with complete faith and encouragement when I first told her about sharing Yield Theory with the world twenty-one years ago.

Appendix A

Essentials of Yield Theory

You will master whatever you practice. If you practice a skill, you will master it. If you practice being angry, you will master that, too. If you practice complaining, you will master that. And this is also true: It's never too late to master something new. So even if you've gotten really good at acting impulsively, it's never too late to start practicing—and mastering—self-control.

Your mind always wants to match your body. In other words, if your body feels anxious, your mind will race to create a story to match what your body is feeling. If your body feels agitated, your mind will quickly search to find a "reason" (or make one up) for why you feel the way you do; and most of the time, that "reason" your mind creates involves something someone else said or did. The more you understand that your mind wants to match your body, the more you can avoid creating a story to match how your body feels.

Every emotional situation has a beginning, a middle, and an end. No matter how bad you feel, ever, no feeling can last forever. There will be a beginning, a middle, and an end to everything you experience. It's wise to avoid making an impulsive decision in the beginning or middle of a tough situation that will leave you with a worse ending.

There is a huge difference between guilt and shame. Guilt is feeling bad about something you've done. Guilt can be a helpful guide to teaching you how to learn from your mistakes. Shame, however, is feeling bad about who you are; and twenty-plus years of experience in the field of counseling have taught me that people who live in shame act out of shame. It's wise to learn how to move beyond shame, because you are not your actions, and as long as you're alive, you have tremendous opportunities to spread kindness and compassion to others.

We would rather be angry than anxious or depressed. It actually feels better to lash out in anger than it does to sit in the awful chemicals that our brains release in anxiety and depression. Unfortunately, after we lash out in anger, we often feel very bad about what we've done. Then we add to the shame we already feel (and remember, those who live in shame act out of shame). The more you understand how to recognize the anxiety and depression that your body feels, the better you can avoid mindlessly lashing out in anger when you're anxious or depressed. It's wise to be mindful about what's really going on with you.

It's perfectly okay to acknowledge or recognize the uncomfortable feelings your body has without reacting to those feelings. The more you learn to be the observer of your feelings, the less obligated you will feel to be a puppet to those feelings. It's wise to remember that every feeling you ever have will eventually pass, so you never need to lash out at others (or yourself) just because you are experiencing uncomfortable temporary emotions.

People see your actions, not your intentions. Interestingly, you judge others by their actions but judge yourself by your intentions. But in life, what you meant to do never matters; only what you actually do matters. Further, we have a tendency to minimize the pain we cause others and maximize the pain others cause us. So if you hurt someone, you think, "What's the big deal? I didn't mean to . . ." But if others hurt you, you think, "I can't believe that person . . ." The wise understand that people only ever see your actions, not your intentions.

The world is not "supposed" to operate according to how you think it "should"; it operates the way it does. There is a difference between the "cartoon world," or the world the way you think it should be, and the "real world," or the world the way it is. The more you expect others and the world to be what you demand they "should" be, the more you will be let down. On the other hand, the more you align your expectations with the reality of how others and the world actually are, the more peace you will find. The wise understand the difference between the unrealistic demands they make in their cartoon worlds and the reality of the world as it actually is.

The more you concentrate on the things you don't like, the more miserable you will be. Conversely, the more you concentrate on peaceful thoughts, the more you will fill your mind with peace. Your mind experiences somewhere on the order of 50,000 to 70,000 thoughts a day, and the thoughts you have affect the way you feel. There is no reason to allow the people and situations you don't like to occupy the majority of your thoughts. The wise understand that your mind will be filled with whatever you put in it, so be mindful to steer yourself toward the type of thoughts that you actually want to fill your mind with.

You will not magically experience internal peace until you work hard at practicing the skills that lead to internal peace. You cannot look at exercise equipment and magically get in shape; you have to actually use the equipment and exercise. Similarly, you are not entitled to have peace without practicing peace. This book offers you many opportunities for such practice. The wise understand that they cannot control the outside world, nor can they always determine what happens to them in life; but they can always control how they respond to what happens to them in life.

To employ Yield Theory, it's essential to practice taking the time to meet people where they are. "Meeting people where they are" means being ready to assess where they actually are in every given second. There's a difference between knowing it's important to meet people where they are and actually doing it.

The best way to teach diverse learners is through diverse creative methods. Whereas it's natural to assume the teaching methods that worked for you will work for others, the reality is that people learn in different ways. The wise know that the most effective way to communicate well is by making an effort to consider the best way that others take in information.

Appendix B

Teaching Tales

Some of these stories I've heard, some I've made up, and still others are based on experiences I've had. All of them are intended to spark insight and awakening. Although the stories are easy to read through quickly, my hope is that you will come back to them time and again until they become a part of you.

Logical Land, Foolish People

▶ Once, a long time ago, a very logical man did some extremely important calculations and reasoning. The people, including the king and queen, anxiously waited to hear what this man had discovered. When his work was completed, he presented his findings to the entire kingdom. So, a crowd gathered, and all were silent. The man exclaimed, "I have discovered that the mountains should not be where they are! If the mountains were precisely one hundred miles south of where they are presently located, all of our problems would be solved!" The crowd erupted in cheers. The king and queen were the first to offer standing ovations, and of course the people followed.

The cheers of the people soon turned to anger, however. A man from the crowd yelled, "He is right! The mountains shouldn't be where they are!" And someone else hollered, "Yes! I see it now! The world is laid out wrong!" Everyone was now angry and distraught at the world for being the way it was. Everyone, that is, except for a little girl.

This girl, this innocent, clear-sighted child, stepped up and said, "But the mountains *are* there. Wouldn't it be better for us to look for other solutions to our problems?" The people laughed at the little girl and said, "What does she know? She's just a child!" And they all turned back to the logical man to hear more about how the earth should be different from how it is. ◀

You, too, can spend your time like the people in this land, unrealistically angry at the world for being the way it is; or you can align your expectations with reality. After all, the more accurately you see the world, the better you will navigate your way through it.

Priceless Lesson

▶ A man walked through an expensive market and grew more and more frustrated as he saw how much the merchants charged for their goods. Finally he got to the king's garden at the end of a row. He took out his money, held it up, and said, "I want to buy four figs." The king's gardener looked at what the man held up and shook his head no. The man grew angry, pulled out more money, and said, "You're all so greedy!" Then he reached into his pocket and pulled out every coin he had. "Here! Here is everything I have! Does it make you happy to milk me dry? I want to buy four figs, and I know this is enough!" But the king's gardener shook his head no again. Just as the man was about to explode with rage, the gardener said, "The king is not a merchant. He does not sell what he has but freely gives it. So no, you may not buy four figs, but yes, you certainly can have them." ◀

When you take old experiences into new situations, you run the risk of bringing unnecessary anger with you. Be mindful not to allow confirmation bias to determine how you approach new experiences. The priceless lesson for you and others is this: The more you expect to see in the world, the less you actually see.

"You Are Not a Pink Elephant!"

▶ A teenager went to the school counselor and said, "I'm so upset. My classmate called me a coward for not wanting to jump off the roof of the school."

The counselor asked, "Did anyone else jump off it?"

The student replied, "No."

"Thank goodness for that! And what a wise choice for you to not jump off a roof!" He paused, then added, "Hey, if I called you a pink elephant, would you be upset?"

The student looked at the counselor as if he were strange. "What?"

"If I called you a pink elephant, would you be upset?"

The student mustered a laugh and said, "No."

"Why not?"

"Because that's ridiculous."

The counselor replied, "You are not a pink elephant! Similarly, you are not a coward. And you are not any other name someone else calls you that doesn't accurately describe you. So if you know you're not a pink elephant and you wouldn't get upset at that, why in the world would you get upset with being called some other name that you're also not?"

The student felt relief. She saw what her counselor was saying and realized it to be true for herself. "I'm not a pink elephant," she thought, "and I'm not a coward either." ◀

The same is true for you. You are not a pink elephant, and you are not anything else you are not. When you understand what you are and what you aren't, you have a significantly easier time refusing to accept others' misinformed definitions of you.

Melting Ice

▶ A boy came home from school distraught. He disclosed his anger at a rising conflict that had been bothering him for weeks. His mother tried to help calm him down, but to no avail. She used to be able to calm him, but this time it was different, and it hurt her to see him struggling like this.

Later that evening, a wandering spiritual teacher came through the town. The mother invited him in, hoping for advice regarding what she considered to be a failure on her part. As she poured hot tea for her guest, she unloaded everything that bothered her about not being able to help her son. The mother wanted to solve her son's conflict quickly, so she was very eager for this man's advice.

Instead of replying to what she asked, however, he seemed to ignore her story and asked her for a small glass of ice. She got it without skipping a beat in her diatribe, handed the teacher the glass of ice, and kept talking, becoming increasingly frustrated as the teacher continued to withhold advice.

Finally he motioned for her to watch what he was doing. He took one piece of ice from the glass and placed it in the hot tea. The mother attempted to keep talking, but he raised a finger for her to be still and pointed to the cup. He picked the tea up to drink it, but made a face demonstrating the tea was too hot. Again, she attempted to talk, but again, he motioned for her to be still, pointed at the tea a second time, and then dropped three more ice cubes in it, one at a time and slowly.

The teacher picked the tea up, drank it easily (since it was now cool), put his cup down, and smiled at her. "Trying to take away emotional pain in minutes that took much longer to develop," he said, "is like putting one ice cube into very hot tea and expecting the tea to be cooled immediately. The hotter the tea, the longer it will take to cool off. That is not a reflection of the ice, but of the heat. The sooner you understand this, the sooner you will bring your son peace." ◄

One ice cube is not enough to cool something that is overly hot, but several ice cubes should do the trick. When you align your expectations with the cartoon world, you might expect that if you listen and validate, others "should" be ready to explore options. But if you're mindful to operate from the real world, you can align your expectations with the reality that it might take longer than you'd like for people to move to the phase where they're exploring options, but it's not the end of the world, and you can certainly handle it.

The more you align your expectation with reality, the more prepared you are for it. Likewise, the more you can make yourself a source of peace, the more peace you can bring to even the highest-conflict situations.

Hell's Half Acre

▶ In the old West, an explorer journeyed past Casper, Wyoming, and found a nearly impassible terrain. The land was extraordinarily difficult for him to cross on foot, let alone with horses, but he ultimately got through it. He named the land Hell's Half Acre. The great thing about this name is that it shows that, no matter how tough the terrain, there will always be a beginning, a middle, and an end to it; it shows that what is nearly impossible is, in fact, possible to get through, which the explorer demonstrated by his actions. ◀

The same is true too for every difficult emotion you (and everyone else) ever experience: It will have a beginning, a middle, and an end. No matter what you go through in life, no matter how difficult, all emotions are temporary; all emotions change. Even if you (or someone you encounter) feel like you're going through hell, the best advice you can follow is to just keep going—because eventually you will get through it.

The Turtle and the Geese

▶ Once there was a turtle who was friends with two geese. The geese invited the turtle to come visit their home. "How can I get there?" he asked. "I don't fly." The geese told him that if he held onto the middle of a stick with his mouth, they would happily carry either end of the stick and fly him there. The turtle agreed.

Along the way, the three passed above some children playing. The children laughed at such a sight. They began to mock the turtle for thinking he could fly. The turtle became furious. "How dare they say those things! They shouldn't talk to me like that!" he thought. And just in the moment when he opened his mouth to set the children straight, he plummeted from the sky to his death. ◀

The turtle didn't expect the reality that occurred; instead, he desired that the children "should" have behaved differently than they did. He felt disrespected and acted out of anger; yet his angry action did nothing to show the children a better path. You might view the turtle as foolish, but you are no different from him when you act out of anger at those who do not behave according to your expectations. When your intentions are to "set others straight" through anger, you are like the turtle who did not know how his desire to change reality would hurt only himself.

All-Consuming Anger

▶ A man was so consumed with anger at his enemy that he vowed to do whatever it took to get even. A strange and mysterious person overheard the angry man's promise and said, "If you really want it badly enough, I can help you." The angry man was obsessed with his thoughts of revenge and demanded that the stranger help him.

The stranger said, "I can teach you one of two paths. If you take the first path, you will absolutely have your revenge, but there is a catch. If you take the second path, your enemy will not be avenged at all, but you will no longer be consumed with anger, only peace."

The angry man immediately asked, "What is the catch with the first path?"

The stranger replied, "The catch is that before your revenge comes to fruition, you yourself will have to die."

The angry man did not even think before he demanded, "Teach it to me! I don't care about a path that doesn't lead to revenge. As long as I get to get even, I don't care what happens to me!" And so it was that his anger harmed him before it ever touched his enemy. ◀

Do your best to avoid being so caught up in your anger that you forget your ultimate goal is to experience peace. Sharing this story with those who are angry can be eye-opening for them, because it can lead to a discussion of the ways in which the people with whom they're angry are controlling them like a puppet and, in a sense, "winning." If what it takes to meet others where they are is to highlight how they are allowing others to have control over them or "win" in some way, then using a story like this can help you bring that kind of awareness. Sometimes bringing an idea like this into a person's foreground is enough to help them alter their course.

Unnecessary Anger

▶ A teenage boy had a crush on a girl who was new to his school. The boy was really insecure, and even though he had never talked to her, he very much wanted to ask her to the upcoming dance. He thought he was going to see her at the beginning of the day, but his classes ran late, and he kept just missing her.

The more time he had to think, the more insecure he became.

He thought, "She probably won't go with me. Who am I kidding? She'll probably think I'm dumb. She probably thinks she's too good for me, anyway." Once he entertained that last thought, it was tough to let it go. All day long, he kept thinking to himself, "She'll never go with me. She'll never go with me. She thinks she's too good for me. She thinks she's too good for me." Those thoughts got louder and louder in his mind.

Finally, at the end of the day, he saw her by his locker. His thoughts had completely gotten the best of him by that time. He walked straight up to her and shouted, "I don't want to go to the stupid dance with you, anyway!" It was the first interaction he'd ever had with her. ◀

Though we've all felt insecurity and we've all created anger stories in our minds, when we witness others' unnecessary anger, we can't help but see the foolishness in it. Learning from others' mistakes via a story like this can help you be more mindful the next time your ego shouts insecure or angry thoughts at you.

Punishing Others Punishes You

▶ A very long time ago, all the different parts of the body were really angry about the unequal distribution of tasks, so they had a meeting to discuss it. You see, some of the body parts were enraged because they felt like they did all the work while the stomach just sat there and reaped the benefits. They decided to revolt. The hands declared that they would no longer bring food to the mouth, the mouth refused to take food in, and the teeth refused to chew anything. They set out to teach the stomach a lesson.

The different body parts convinced themselves that they were punishing the stomach. However, it did not take long for the whole body to begin to weaken and waste away.

The body parts came together for a second meeting. This time the aim of the meeting was to apologize to the stomach. They offered gratitude for the digestion and distribution that it carries out for the whole body. ◄

Just because you cannot immediately see the value that others bring doesn't mean it's not there. The hatred you extend to others will most often hurt you the most. The more you can see the interconnectedness of everyone and the role everyone in your life plays in the story of who you are (including teaching you motivation, patience, how to overcome obstacles, and other invaluable lessons), the more you will understand the reality that punishing others punishes you.

Learning from Anger

▶ Once a man came to the master, enraged. The man said that he was furious with his boss and that his anger was so overwhelming, it took him every ounce of control not to do something regretful. The teacher praised the man's restraint, but the man only replied that he thought he had progressed further in his path to peace, and he was surprised by how overcome with anger he was. "I am still so angry! I want to leave that job, but I don't know if I should! I don't want to work somewhere where people act like that! But I don't know what to do . . ."

The teacher listened until the man was finished, and then he spoke. "Imagine your anger is a kind, old, wise, and balanced friend who just wants to give you an important message right now. What do you think that message might be?"

The man thought about it for a bit. The more he thought about it, the more calm he became. Finally he said, "To leave my job."

"And you would be okay if you did?" asked the teacher.

"Yes, I really would," said the man, much more calmly.

The teacher smiled at him. "Sounds like you're ready to thank Anger. Only a moment ago you were uncertain about what to do, but your wise friend Anger has given you direction."

The man sat for a moment. He was entirely calm now. He smiled and realized that his anger was there to teach him and that he was now at peace with his decision to leave his job. ◄

Consider personifying your emotions as older, wiser companions (because personifying something like anger without intentionally visualizing through the lens of wisdom might result in you picturing an impulsive teenager egging you on to make reckless decisions). By visualizing your emotions as wise leaders in your life, you can learn from them. In other words, when the moment comes, you can be angry with Anger or you can learn from it, but the choice will always be yours.

Get to Rigel

▶ Orion is one of the most easily recognizable constellations in the sky. Of all the arbitrary stars that make up Orion, the one named Rigel is the brightest. A fascinating reality is that if you were to travel to Rigel, you would not be able to see the constellation Orion, just as we cannot see the myriad of potential constellations in which our own sun resides.

The constellation Orion does not visibly exist from everywhere, and neither do your problems. Seen from multiple vantage points, your own problems can morph, shrink, and even disappear. ◄

From the vantage point of your ego, problems are huge; travel to your authentic core, however, and all of a sudden problems like pride disappear altogether. If you're stuck in anger, get to Rigel. If you want to help others get unstuck, help them travel to Rigel.

Using your creativity in situations of conflict, whether it's through experiential exercises, metaphors, or teaching tales, is like opening a wormhole that can help people make the jump from anger to insight quickly, even if feels like it's light-years away.

God's Job

▶ In the olden days, God lived among the people. He couldn't stay living there, though, because everyone in the land constantly bothered him day and night. They would knock on his door at all hours, complaining to him to do this or that: "Make it rain!" or "Stop the floods!" and every other demand as well.

One day, a farmer went to God and said, "Look, let me have your job, because I could end world hunger." God thought that sounded nice, and he was tired of being harassed, so he let the farmer have at it.

The farmer made it rain only the perfect amount of moisture. He brought out the sun just the perfect amount of time. He made the weather perfect all the time, in fact, and the wheat grew so high that it looked like there would be food for everyone for the next ten years. But then, when the wheat was harvested, the people found that there was nothing but inedible chaff. The farmer asked God what happened. God said, "Because there was no challenge, no obstacle, no conflict, no difficulty, the wheat could not grow properly. A little struggle is a must. You need the storms. You need the thunder, the lightning. You need the conflict—it's the only way growth happens." ◀

Whatever you're experiencing is necessary. You need to be going through exactly what you're going through, because the conflict you're in right now and the way you handle it is shaping the person you're about to become. The same is true for others. The more you embrace where you are, as well as the perspective that encompasses why you are where you are, the better chance you have to move through what you're experiencing in the most conscious way possible.

Give Me Your Temper

▶ A student went to the master and told her how troubled he was by his temper. "I can't control it. It controls me. I don't want this temper anymore."

The master smiled at the student and said, "Give me your temper, and I will fix it for you."

But the student was confused and said, "I cannot give you my temper, because my temper is not a thing."

And the master asked, "If your temper is no-thing, then how can it control you?"

Immediately, the student became enlightened. From that moment on, he understood that his temper would only ever be what he made it to be. ◀

The Buddha taught that all problems arise from the mind. The philosopher Ludwig Wittgenstein declared that there are no real problems in life, only problems in language. Whether these descriptions resonate with you or not, one thing that's difficult to deny is the power and impact that the language of your self-talk has as it moves through your mind. Anger isn't tangible until you act on it.

Samurai Strength

▶ A king called on his best samurai warrior to track down and kill his enemy. The samurai did so. He found the enemy, and he bested him quickly. Just as the samurai was about to kill the man, however, the enemy spit right in the samurai's face. The samurai warrior paused, stepped back, and sheathed his sword.

Instead of killing the man, he brought him before the king. The king said, "I commanded you to kill him, not capture him!"

The samurai replied, "My king, you commanded me to kill him, but when he spit in my face it angered me, and I realized that if I killed him in that moment, I would have done so out of anger and not out of duty." ◀

The samurai had worked too hard on his self-control to allow impulse to defeat him. True toughness is being able to control yourself, not others.

I use this story to help meet those stuck in anger where they are. Understanding that people associate anger with toughness is important in conflict situations. In my experience, the symbol of the samurai is universally respected, so drawing on stories of samurai warriors is a fast path to reaching people who are struggling to maintain control. The samurai are respected because of their incredible skills and ability to defend themselves. There is no denying that they have earned the respect of others who want to be looked at similarly. I've watched countless people respond really well to hearing this and similar stories.

Box Head

▶ A teacher was asked by his student in class what the ego is like. The teacher looked around the room and spotted a cardboard box filled with papers and old magazines. He picked the box up, dumped its contents onto the floor, then turned the box upside down over his head. He hollered, "I know where I'm going!" as he walked right into the wall.

The students laughed. He did it again. They laughed with a little less intensity.

The teacher shouted it once more and pretended to walk into the wall a third time. This time, there were only courtesy laughs from a couple of students. One student, trying to get a laugh of his own from the group, said, "It's not funny anymore." The students laughed.

The teacher took the box off his head and said, "That's what the ego is like: It boxes in your vision, convinces you that you know more than you do, and makes you self-centered in a way that quickly gets tiring to others."

The student who had asked the question understood. They all understood. And all who were present strove from that day onward to never be a "box head" again. ◀

When you understand how this story applies to your own life, it makes you all the more credible as you share it with others. The "box head" limits us; the recognition of its limits frees us.

Peace Takes Practice

▶ Once there were two aliens who came to Earth. Their spaceships landed at the same time and in the same way, but in two different houses. Both aliens landed in English-speaking homes where the people were willing to teach them the language. But wow! They experienced two entirely different reactions.

The first alien landed in a home where the people spoke in extremes. "This is terrible!" the family said. "We can't believe this is our terrible luck!" Everything they taught the alien was couched in extreme adjectives. "Nothing's fair! Why did you have to land here? Now we have to spend our money on feeding you!" they complained. The alien soon learned how to complain, too. He learned how to exaggerate everything that happened. He learned how to express discontent with everything. After all, he did not know the language until he met this family.

Ultimately, he learned that he was a terrible bother to the humans, and he felt awful and guilty and terrible. He really disliked this planet; all he wanted to do was leave. The humans didn't realize that their own words and actions were making him feel awful. When he wanted to leave, they complained more: "Look how ungrateful the alien is! After everything we did for him, too!" The alien couldn't wait to go.

The other alien landed in a home where gratitude was all the family expressed. "Thank you for landing on our home!" they said. "Thank you for showing us that there is life out there!" The family spoke with gratitude about everything. This second alien, in turn, learned how to speak in gratitude. Because he learned peaceful dialogue, he learned to feel peace. The alien felt welcomed in this home and hoped to stay forever. The family was happy. The alien was happy.

Sure, the world isn't perfect, but it's not supposed to be. All we can ever do is hope to talk to ourselves in the way that helps us best. ◀

How you talk about the world is how you will experience the world. If you find yourself angry more than you want to be, consider reevaluating the type of self-talk you have. The more balanced and accurate your self-talk, the more likely you are to find peace.

About the Author

Dr. Christian Conte is a licensed professional counselor and world-renowned anger management specialist. He specializes in working with people convicted of violent crimes. He is an author, speaker, and radio and television personality. In addition to the work he does in prisons and consulting for top organizations, Dr. Conte also works with some of the most elite athletes and top athletic teams in the country. He and his beautiful wife, Kristen, have been happily married for nineteen years, and their incredible daughter, Kaia, is their pride and joy. They live in Southwestern Pennsylvania.

About Sounds True

Sounds True is a multimedia publisher whose mission is to inspire and support personal transformation and spiritual awakening. Founded in 1985 and located in Boulder, Colorado, we work with many of the leading spiritual teachers, thinkers, healers, and visionary artists of our time. We strive with every title to preserve the essential "living wisdom" of the author or artist. It is our goal to create products that not only provide information to a reader or listener, but that also embody the quality of a wisdom transmission.

For those seeking genuine transformation, Sounds True is your trusted partner. At SoundsTrue.com you will find a wealth of free resources to support your journey, including exclusive weekly audio interviews, free downloads, interactive learning tools, and other special savings on all our titles.

To learn more, please visit SoundsTrue.com/freegifts or call us toll-free at 800.333.9185.

sounds true
WAKING UP THE WORLD